Systematic Theology
through the
Spiritual Eye

Volume IV
Introduction, Hybrid, School Interaction
Walking Your Vision University/
Academy

Apostle Charles Frederick Tolbert,
DivM, EdM, EdD, PhD, Retired US Army

ISBN 979-8-89428-446-0 (paperback)
ISBN 979-8-89428-447-7 (digital)

Copyright © 2024 byApostle Charles Frederick Tolbert, DivM, EdM, EdD, PhD, Retired US Army

All rights reserved. No part of this publication may be reproduced, distributed, or transmitted in any form or by any means, including photocopying, recording, or other electronic or mechanical methods without the prior written permission of the publisher. For permission requests, solicit the publisher via the address below.

Christian Faith Publishing
832 Park Avenue
Meadville, PA 16335
www.christianfaithpublishing.com

Printed in the United States of America

To all ministries in 195 counties and territories.

CONTENTS

PRAYER FOR THE PEACE OF THE WORLD

A prayer for the peace of the world.

In the name of the Father and of the Son and of the Holy Spirit. Amen.

O Lord, our God, who can be compared with you? Who is even similar to you among the gods? What god is as great as our God, who is abundant in mercy and benevolent in strength to bring consolation and salvation to all of us? This is why we pray to you, O God, this day, not be silent at a time when we hear the sounds of war and threats from the mighty ones of the earth.

Forgive, O most loving God, forgive and show mercy. You are a most compassionate and merciful Lord, and you will not chastise us in your wrath nor instruct us in your anger. Otherwise, we would revert to the chaos at the beginning before we came into existence. During these difficult times, be with us. Lord, our God, make us strong, for we have placed our hope in you and are fortified in and encouraged by your name. May your word be confirmed, Lord, which you spoke to us that you will be with us always even to the end of the age.

May the hopes of the Christians be raised up high, and may those who threaten us be put to shame. May those who threaten us with wars and battles be terrified, shamed, and scattered, and may their power be destroyed and their dominion be no more. And they will all know indeed that your name is the Lord, that you alone are the Most High over all the earth. Hear the voice of our supplicant, O Lord, and turn away from us the dangers that threaten the human race, dissolve the clouds of devastation from a possible war, and solidify your peace among us so that your all-holy name will be glorified, in the name of the Father, the Son, and the Holy Spirit, now and ever and unto ages of ages. Amen.

THE PURPOSE OF CFACS INC.
(CHRIST FOUND ALL CREATION SAVED)

Global virtual reality (live streaming through interaction) hybrid schools/universities are to teach and train every student in the philosophy of life through the logos of the ever-living Father. Second Timothy 2:15 (KJV) states, "Be diligent to present yourself approved to God, a worker who does not need to be ashamed, rightly dividing the word of truth" and to the heirs of the promise. And if you are Christ's, then you are Abraham's seed and heirs according to the promise (Galatians 3:29).

The mission of CFACS Inc. Waking Your Vision Academy/University is to go into the entire world, teaching the gospel of Jesus Christ, baptizing them in the name of the Father, Son, and Holy Spirit and in the name of Jesus.

And he said to them, "Go into all the world and preach the gospel to every creature. He who believes and is baptized will be saved; but he who does not believe will be condemned. And these signs will follow those who believe in my name they will cast out demons; they will speak with new tongues; they will take up serpents; and if they drink anything deadly, it will by no means hurt them; they will lay hands on the sick, and they will recover" (Mark 16:15–18).

And then they heard that they were baptized in the name of the Lord Jesus and be baptized in the Holy Spirit, speaking in tongues according to Jesus's commandment (Acts 19:5).

> Behold, I send the promise of my father upon you; but tarry in the city of Jerusalem until you are endued with the power from high. (Luke 24:49)

And being assembled together with them, he commanded them not to depart from Jerusalem but to wait for the promise of the Father, which he said, "You have heard from me…for John truly baptized with water but you shall be baptized with the Holy Spirit not too many days from now" (Acts 1:4–5).

> And they were all filled with the Holy Spirit and began to speak with other tongues, as the Spirit gave them utterance. (Acts 2:4)

The results of CFACS Academy are that the sons of God be equipped spiritually, mentally, and physically to set creation free, as was prophesied in the second chapter of Joel.

> They run like mighty men, they climb the wall like men of war; They do not push one another; everyone marches

in his own column. Though they lunge between the weapons, they run not cut down. They run to and from in the city, they run on wall, They climb into the houses, They enter at the windows like a thief. The earth quakes before them, the heavens tremble; The sun and moon grow dark, And the stars diminish their brightness. The Lord gives voices before His army. For His camp is very great; For strong is the One who executes His word, For the day of the Lord is great and very terrible; Who can endure it? (Joel 2:7–11)

Likewise the Spirit also helpeth our infirmities: for we know not what we should pray for as we ought: but the Spirit itself maketh intercession for us with groanings which cannot be uttered. Now He who searches the hearts knows what the mind of the Spirit is, because He makes intercession for saints according to the will of God. (Romans 8:26–27)

Apostle Charles Frederick Tolbert is currently teaching internationally with the long-term goal of establishing virtual reality (live streaming through interaction) hybrid school systems.

Dr. Tolbert's intention is to bring ministries into a global virtual reality (live streaming through interaction) hybrid school/university system, where there is homeschooling, teaching in the assembly, and combining it in the classrooms with on-the-job training. Walking Your Vision University teaching is systematic theology. There are 195 countries that he intends to expand the training within five to ten years.

> Behold, I will send my messenger, and he shall prepare the way before me: and the Lord, whom ye seek, shall suddenly come to his temple, even the messenger of the covenant, whom ye delight in: behold, he shall come, saith the Lord of hosts. (Malachi 3:1)

A certificate of graduation is to be presented to students who have completed the course outline in the book *Systematic Theology through the Spiritual Eye* and have presented a five-page (font 10) paper outlining what they have learned by reading the book.

The university will cover the following:

- Be responsible for providing quality instruction to students through well-prepared classes, relevant assignments, fair and holistic assessment of learning, clear documentation of student progress, and support of the academic success for at-risk students, teach assigned courses

- Adequately prepare all course materials and lessons (Note: Preparation time will vary based on instructor experience in teaching that course.)
- Provide each student with clear course expectations, evaluations, and time lines through carefully written topical outlines and approved, standardized syllabus.
- Provide interesting and relevant assignments for students that demonstrate learning outcomes in a real-life setting
- Suitably challenge, engage, serve, and communicate with students to encourage their participation and learning while maintaining mutual value and respect
- Complete grade books, final grade sheets, learning assessments, and final exam assessments on a timely basis
- Respond to student questions on a timely basis
- Identify and refer at-risk students to specific academic support services
- Ensure course and program-learning outcomes are delivered as defined by the syllabus
- Act as a substitute as needed
- Attend graduation ceremonies each year
- Ensure safety and sanitation of all labs, equipment, and supplies where applicable
- Post and maintain office and classroom schedules
- Participate in and provide feedback to institutional committees and reporting
- Work with program chair and other appropriate groups on retention activities
- Provide mentoring to new faculty

- Assist director of education in program evaluation and planning
- Attend regularly scheduled in-services and discipline-specific professional development activities
- Be responsible in maintaining credentials as required by accrediting councils/agencies and regulatory bodies

Investigating the Feasibility of Replicating Existing Traditional Accredited Parochial Schools into a Hybrid Educational System

A Concept Paper Submitted to the
in Partial Fulfillment of the Requirements for
the Degree of Doctor of Education 2010

Apostle Charles Frederick Tolbert
DivM, EdM, EdD, PhD

INTRODUCTION

For the purposes of this paper, a hybrid school system will be defined as schools that use classroom, online sources, and homeschooling to teach the accredited curriculum. This replication will happen regardless of the main school's location, and this initiative reflects the directions of education systems in the future. The changing global education system requires that new innovative instructions be researched for all grade levels in order for parochial schools to compete with the traditional public school system.

The introduction of technology web-based teachings and its integration into nonprofit organizations to include physical places of worship have enabled outreach programs to be expanded outside of the assemblies to the four corners of God's arrangement. This paper will explore the concept of curriculum evaluation, looking at the issues of integrating technology into Community Assistance Programs (CAP) and teaching men responsibility and formal biblical instructions. The major concerns are location of the information technology department (ITD); use of resource (money, time, and personnel) to support technology; and the educating of men, women, and children using multimedia and technology with and availability of access to teachers for the hybrid school system. There is a belief that technology will cause changes in the way secular schools teach, and religious-based schools might want to consider the cause and effect of money being spent to maintain and operate a school building. Ginsburg (1999) stated, "We all acknowledge that the information age has had a profound impact on the world around us; thus it is not unreasonable to assume that the information age should also affect the form and function of adult education" (p. 45).

With regard to integrating biblical studies into the curriculum, from the spiritual perspective, all books in the Bible should be read not by the words written but the relationship of the words as discerned by one's own spirit after prayers, fasts, and supplicates. According to Fenton (1996), "Every Divinely inspired and useful writing was intended for teaching, attestation, and education in righteousness, so that the man of God might be noble, and well trained for every good work" (p. 1231).

Research problem and purpose for benchmark of accredited parochial schools

The problem is, it is unknown if it is feasible to replicate existing traditional accredited parochial schools into a hybrid educational system within a five-year period. The primary question is whether it is feasible to replicate these existing parochial schools into a hybrid system, and can it be accomplished in five years? This paper will include a benchmark of accredited parochial schools that will serve as a pattern for the restructuring of parochial schools into hybrid parochial schools.

Included agencies and documentation will present information that will support the hybrid school system. Other parochial schools will also be compared with and contrasted to charter schools. Funding and curriculum will be the two major problems. The problem is the mandate by the federal government for the public school system to remove God from all aspects of education.

The nature of the problem is that the target academy is being challenged to develop a hybrid school parochial school for the staff and board of directors. The purpose of the evaluation is to design and develop a program evaluation plan for the target academy to determine whether the media usage and curriculum meet the requirements and the directives of the academy. Further, the purpose is to determine the feasibility of the academy becoming accredited (K–12) in five years. The evaluation is to provide information for instructing students using multimedia.

Five research questions will be examined in this study:

1. What will be the appropriate program evaluation plan for the target academy?
2. What will be an appropriate hybrid parochial school and valid format for development of program evaluation plan for the target academy?
3. Does the curriculum meet the requirements established by the stakeholders?
4. Can the target academy submit and receive accreditation within five years?

5. Which of the traditions by Creswell (2003) will be used for the collection of information?

In answering the main questions, the following questions become important parts of the qualitative question:

1. Will low-literacy learners be able to learn effectively using the computer?
2. How can the computer aid to promote learning?
3. Is the staff able to continue to develop a curriculum that meets the ministry's teaching requirements?
4. Will the production department be able to meet the demand of producing the required CDs and meet the shipping quota?
5. Have other ministries been able to provide teaching using online and in-class techniques?
6. Will resultant teaching empower men to be more responsible?
7. Can the program be expanded into the correctional facilities?
8. Does online teaching meet the state accreditation school requirements?
9. Can one or more instructors effectively teach twelve students in a three-hour block in a traditional setting?
10. Will the lesson plans, rubric, and other curriculum-related material require continuous review?
11. Should the mission statement be changed, and if yes, what would be an appropriate suggestion?

12. Can other not-for-profit organizations replicate the hybrid parochial system?
13. If a template for submission to procure accreditation to the state for K–12 were available to your organization, would you start a parochial school? If so, why? And if not, why not?

Of these thirteen subquestions, question 13 will be used for the purpose of this dissertation. Question 5 is being addressed in this paper in order to provide the reader with an understanding of how the writer will choose and implement two of the traditions by Creswell (2003).

Through a set of procedures, a development plan for a hybrid parochial school is being developed for the target academy. Subject experts in the field and their information are being considered. Training objectives will be established by a committee representing the target academy and South Florida–area professionals. At the conclusion of the process, the target academy will offer the results to the board of directors and to additional stakeholders. The recommendation will be to offer this evaluation concerning curriculum on an ongoing basis as a means of continuous review and updating as required.

Needs assessment, purpose, and goals

The existing academy is a nonprofit 501c3 place of worship. Students are admitted regardless of race, creed, color, and religious or sexual preference from the age of eighteen and older. Currently, the academy operates on a fifty-two-week calendar that is delivered both online and at the physical location as a hybrid system. There are no physical requirements or educational limitations.

The teachers hired to work with these students must be graduates of the academy, either through the online course or at the school's designated location. It is preferred that all teachers also have a background in computers and online teaching.

According to Boffetti (nd), parents want more than just good grades too; they think moral instruction is important. Many parents send their children to private religious schools at their own expense or educate their children at home. In fact, almost all parents believe that their children need such instruction. More than 90 percent of parents believe that *schools* ought to try to instill the virtues of honesty and moral courage, apply the golden rule, teach children to accept people with different ethnic and religious backgrounds, and promote democracy. And 68 percent of parents want schools to teach sexual abstinence (p. 1).

Nature of the problem

The nature of the problem is, will the resultant template, appropriate for submission to the state, be attractive to other schools and institutions? Subsequently, would these other schools and institutions actually institute a hybrid parochial school? Lastly, if so, why? And if not, why not?

Students seeking to be ordained as ministers will need to complete the web-based school, along with listening to fifty-five CDs and the reading of the Bible provided as part of the course of study to fulfill the mandate by the target academy. They will have a comprehensive understanding of the books of the Bible. The target academy has both on-site (limited to twelve students once a week for two hours for fifty-two weeks) courses and an unlimited number of students online. In addition, the target academy is considering the establishment of a parochial school that can be replicated by other not-for-profit organizations. The perspective resulted from a request for developing a program evaluation plan and to solicit responses from other ministries using two of the five traditions by Creswell (2003). The two traditions being used for this study are the ground theory and case study.

Purpose of the development of a program evaluation plan

The purpose of this development study is to design and develop a program evaluation plan for the target academy. This evaluation plan will provide information that will lead to better practices and policies. Educational evaluation is clearly decision oriented. It is intended to lead to better policies and practices in education (Wolf 1990). According to Herod (2000), "discussions are commonly framed against the related notions of formative and summative purposes, terms first used by Scriven in 1967" (p. 23). Herod also wrote, "In determining the value of curriculum plan, educators must eventually ask if the results which are expected, are worth what the cost of delivering them is likely to be" (p. 23). Herod further stated, "Front-end evaluation would allow adult literacy practitioners to clarify, make decisions, and act on the issues rather than fall victim to the steamroller that is technology" (p. 23).

Why program is being evaluated

The program is being evaluated, and the nature of the problem is that the target academy is being challenged to develop a program evaluation plan for the staff and board of directors. The purpose of the evaluation is to design the program evaluation plan for the target academy to determine whether the media usage and curriculum meet the requirements and the directives of the academy. The evaluation is to provide information for instructing students using multimedia.

What is the structure and context of the program?

The structure and context of the program is the introduction of technology web-based teachings and its integration into nonprofit organizations to include physical places of worship, enabling outreach programs to be expanded outside of the assemblies to the four corners of God's arrangement. This paper explores the concept of curriculum evaluation, looking at the issues of integrating technology into CAP, teaching adults and children responsibility, and formal biblical wisdom. The major concerns are location of the ITD; use of resources (money, time, and personnel) to support technology; and the educating of men, women, and children.

HYBRID LEARNING IS QUICKLY BECOMING ONE OF THE MOST IMPORTANT TEACHINGS

Hybrid learning is quickly becoming one of the most important teaching methods to use. Because it is associated strongly with technology, it may be scary to adapt this change, especially if you already are already facing other challenges in the classroom.

Knowing how to set up your hybrid learning space is key for not only avoiding future issues, but also, it is essential for enhanced student-centered learning. Thanks to reliable EdTech and strategic classroom design, hybrid learning is made easy. With these strategies and design, your hybrid learning space is going to be optimized.

Read on to learn more about hybrid learning and the hybrid learning space or see ViewSonic's hybrid learning solutions.

Hybrid learning is a newer teaching strategy using technology. Because many modern classrooms now use technology, teachers are coming up with new ways to shift the paradigms of education so that they are more student centered. A part of this paradigm change is hybrid learning.

Hybrid learning is beneficial to all kinds of students. Whether they are receiving special education, are A-plus students, or are the lovable troublemaker, hybrid learning offers a solution for them. Most importantly, hybrid learning offers flexible teaching strategies and classroom setups for teachers.

A part of this hybrid strategy is to know how to format your students' learning spaces. This is important because half, if not more, of your students are not physically present in the classroom. Without proper classroom design, distanced students will be bored, perform poorly, and potentially even fall behind. Thankfully, we have some tips and suggestions for you!

Brief introduction to hybrid learning

Hybrid learning is a type of blended learning that refers to implementing synchronous lessons that are taught simultaneously in person and online.

Hybrid learning is great because it allows the children who need face-to-face instruction to receive that while those who desire a more flexible approach can receive that as well. Hybrid learning also allows for varying teaching strategies to be used with only a fraction of the challenge.

You can also learn more about synchronous and asynchronous learning here: "Asynchronous vs Synchronous Learning" What's Best for Distance Education?

Why Are Hybrid Learning Spaces Beneficial?

Hybrid learning is beneficial for several reasons. One of the most bragged-about reasons hybrid learning is encouraged is that it increases flexibility for students. This is because flexibility is an important part of a student's learning experience. Whether it be for pacing issues, scheduling due to family matters, chronic illnesses, or other factors, hybrid learning closes the gap for these students.

But flexibility is just one of the many benefits of hybrid learning. Some of these include more inclusive classrooms, student-centered pedagogy, increased student collaboration, active learning, and so much more!

How to set up hybrid learning spaces

Hybrid learning seems great on paper, but there are some challenges you should consider when adapting to a hybrid learning strategy. The biggest factor is the learning spaces involved and how to utilize them productively. Learning spaces for hybrid learning should consider not only the physical location but how these physical locations interact and build upon one another.

Hybrid learning at home

Creating a hybrid learning space at home is probably one of the more difficult learning spaces to set up. You as a parent or a teacher offering suggestions must consider what is the best option for the student. For example, if the student has poor microphone quality or video quality, then it can be difficult to be heard or seen in the physical classroom and so on.

Ensure, at the bare minimum, that your student has a decent computer and a functioning Internet connection so that they will not be left behind in class, and consult with all students about what their capabilities are. Do not use lessons that can only be done with one type of technology. Always be considerate of accessibility, as well as the living situation for the student.

What is also important for the home learning space is where you choose to learn. Let the student pick the spot that is most comfortable to them. Whether it is near a noisy window or a peaceful corner, they know where they feel more comfortable and productive. Khan Academy provided seven tips for setting up a productive learning space at home if you'd like to learn more!

Hybrid learning in the classroom

Hybrid learning in the classroom means deciding what technology you will use. It also may involve determining if this subject is really fit for hybrid situations. Some lessons can only be taught face-to-face; however, most can be adapted and modified to hybrid learning environments.

After you have set up the frameworks, you can start to consider the technology you need. However, there are three main technologies your classroom will need for successful hybrid learning.

INTERACTIVE WHITEBOARD

Interactive whiteboards are a catch-all term for interactive touch displays that respond to real-time action and act like traditional whiteboards. Every classroom needs a chalkboard or a whiteboard, but transforming it into the digital is highly important. With a high-functioning and high-quality interactive whiteboard with the right software, you can promote student collaboration, share content, use remote teaching strategies, and so much more on a single device.

If you are looking for a high-functioning and high-quality interactive whiteboard with preinstalled software, check out websites.

Video hardware and software

Having good video recording or live streaming hardware is extremely important for hybrid learning spaces. Since half or more of your students will be presented on video, one of the biggest challenges of hybrid learning is getting everyone to hear one another, canceling out noise, and loss of connection.

To help solve this issue, purchase laptops, interactive whiteboards, or other hardware with built-in microphones, as well as consider investing in professional external microphones if you are using recordings. You can also use external screens and use a projector so that all in-class students can easily see distanced students clearly.

If you are interested in a projector, check out how to choose the perfect education projector or learn more on why videos are so important in hybrid learning with video-assisted learning.

ViewSonic has developed the myViewBoard Suite, a group of apps designed to facilitate learning in a broad number of configurations. For a hybrid learning space, myViewBoard Classroom has been specifically developed with a number of tools to ensure students get the most out of each lesson.

Assistive technology

One of the benefits of hybrid learning is the ability to create more inclusive classrooms. This is because we can utilize more types of assistive technologies in the classroom or make lessons available to students who have difficulty being physically present in the classroom. Assistive technology is defined as any device, piece of equipment, or system that helps to enhance and accommodate people with special needs, impairments, or disabilities.

Assistive technology, in this case, can be the laptops, video equipment, or other technologies you use to include students with certain needs into your classroom. Not to mention, the ViewBoard has functions like live-closed captions, recording, screen sharing, and other functions to easily modify your lesson plans to fit all students, whether they are distanced or in class.

If you'd like to learn more about assistive technology for all kinds of situations, you can learn more by reading and learning.

HYBRID LEARNING AS A WORKSPACE

The final hybrid learning space you need to consider is the workspace. The workspace, in this sense, refers to how students will work and collaborate with one another. This means targeting more of the classroom design rather than the hardware required. However, you should consider your and your students' hardware and software when creating an optimal classroom design for collaboration between students.

Think-pair-share is one of the most common group collaboration strategies around. This strategy requires a few minutes of individual thinking, pairing two or more students, and then sharing ideas among themselves. The benefit of this is that it is easy to pair distance students with in-class students. You can even mute the distanced students for them to discuss among themselves or other variants of the process.

When deciding on this classroom design, you can use traditional design formats. This can be all desks facing the front toward a screen. You can also consider using varieties of what are called upgraded classrooms. However, these kinds of set up are best suited for schools that can have access to tablets or laptops for individual students.

This form of collaborative strategy relies on students building upon each other to create the final concept. The two teams are broken into what are called "home" and "experts." To use a method in groups, one or more students who are the experts will leave their group, collect information on a particular topic, then return to their home group to share. Once discussion has finished, all groups will share and collaborate to finish.

When setting up a classroom for jigsaw strategies, it would be best to have two displays of some kind, whether it is two interactive whiteboards or two projectors. Place in-class students in the middle, while the distance students will be on the outside or projected on the wall. That way, everyone is visible in various directions.

Different is unique in that it can use both strategies of think-pair-share and jigsaw. However, it focuses highly on discussion and creativity. You bowl for several different reasons, such as text readings, discussion, collaborative problem-solving, and more. Most importantly, it is a fun way to encourage students to communicate and not to be shy when sharing their ideas.

Different may be more difficult to design in hybrid learning as it is meant to be in a circle or "campfire." However, if you have multiple classroom tablets, or if all students have a cell phone or other video/microphone technologies, each distance student can be paired with an in-class student. There are multiple different ways you could emulate in your hybrid learning workspace.

Final considerations for hybrid learning spaces

Hybrid learning spaces are ideal for a multitude of scenarios. So if you ever feel your setup or strategy is not working, try another one! Hybrid learning allows teachers and students to have more freedom and options in their learning and teaching experiences.

If you would like more information on how hybrid learning can benefit your students or would like to contact us for more information on how to get accessible EdTech solutions, visit our hybrid learning education solutions page to get all that and more. Or learn more about the distance learning component of hybrid learning here.

ANOTHER EXAMPLE IS
HYBRID LEARNING

Hybrid learning refers to an approach in which a group of students participate online, while others are taught on campus. This means that the instructor is teaching both remote and in-person students at the same time.

Many people might use the words *hybrid* and *blended* interchangeably, but in fact, they mean different things. That difference lies primarily upon the proportion of face-to-face, online sessions, or instructional materials provided in a course.

Read more about online, hybrid, blended, and Hyflux learning.

Why hybrid learning

Studies have been conducted on the effectiveness of hybrid learning, with the majority highlighting the great benefits presented to institutions, instructors, and learners. And here are the advantages of hybrid learning:

1. Flexibility of course design

Hybrid learning offers the best of both worlds, as it harnesses the unique advantages of each approach: face-to-face (FTF) and online instruction—that is, faculties can generate a flexible, personalized learning experience by making use of both online and FTF resources (learning activities, study materials, and assessment) to address the varied learning barriers and needs of students. Hybrid learning allows for flexibility in learning schedule, teaching approaches, how students interact with the study materials, and in communication with peers and their instructor.

2. Increase of students' satisfaction, engagement, and retention

Students prefer hybrid instruction to online and FTF learning, as many researches show. In hybrid courses, students are presented with more instructional strategies and resources, also greater opportunities to engage in meaningful conversations. This critically enhances learners' satisfaction and engagement throughout the course, leading to a higher level of performance in final assessment.

3. Enhancement of motivation, engagement, and interaction

Hybrid learning allows students to learn anytime, anywhere, and at their own pace. Furthermore, pedagogical technology enables the creation of highly interactive, engaging course materials and activities, which stimulate active learning and engagement among the students. For example, prerecorded lectures enriched with questions or discussions encourage students to really follow the lessons and to engage in conversations with others to develop deep understanding.

4. Nurture of career-ready skills

> Honing lifelong skills should hold as much importance in the curriculum as discipline-specific content. ("Quality Online Teaching and Learning")

More and more universities have been moving away from exam-oriented, rigid curricula toward the pedagogical approaches that center career readiness and lifelong skills. Lifelong skills such as critical thinking, collaboration, and communication, while not always directly related to the core learning content, have an overwhelmingly positive impact on students' performance and are deemed essential to future professional success.

Hybrid learning is among the delivery modes that help cultivate a multitude of tangible skills. Exposure to eLearning materials and learning activities stimulates the development of research skills, self-direction, decision-making, and technology literacy. As hybrid instruction allows for creation of activities where students need to work together to produce a project, skills such as teamwork, problem-solving, and communication have the place to thrive.

How to prepare for hybrid learning

With the rise of hybrid learning, institutions face the challenge of delivering effective, engaging lessons for both in-person and online learners. Instructors, therefore, are in high need of professional training, effective practices, and teaching communities in hybrid and online course design. Furthermore, considerations should be made in terms of space, learning and teaching design, teacher readiness, and support system.

- Focus on cultivating a learning community.
- Prioritize creating meaningful interactions and dialogues within the hybrid classroom with engaging learning activities, clear instructions, and continuous feedback.
- Develop a shared vocabulary of online/hybrid instruction.
- Practice a universal understanding of online and hybrid instruction-enhanced teacher-student communication when it comes to delivering course expectations.
- Be selective in curriculum planning and development.
- Decide on the most important content to cover and design a handful of highly engaged activities with the support of pedagogical tools.
- Advocate for inclusive course design.

Hybrid learning allows institutions to address accessibility and diversity. Adopting inclusive course design and universal design for learning (UDL) is then a must.

FOUR TIPS TO PREPARE FOR HYBRID TEACHING: HOW TO SET UP A HYBRID CLASSROOM

Creating a successful course—whether face-to-face, online, or hybrid—requires a lot more thought than merely producing study materials and assigning work to students. Think of the course design process as building a house. Though different house types (course design formats) require different procedure, they all come down to these six basic steps:

Step 1: Establish clear objectives and expectations.

Instructors need to think about the course type, host platform, teaching tools, and most importantly, the course objectives. Course objectives will act as the North Star for your entire course development process, as all learning activities and assessment practices will be derived from them.

Here are some resources for creating clear, effective learning objectives:

1. The Bloom's taxonomy and its associated verbs are very useful tools for setting up course objectives.

2. The SMART criteria is also a wonderful framework to help you define the objectives for your students.

Step 2: Decide on the teaching approaches.

Hybrid learning, with the combination of both online and FTF instruction, can accommodate and optimize plenty of learning methods, such as collaborative learning, problem-based learning, or social learning. Introducing a variety of teaching approaches to your classrooms is the key to nurture lifelong learning, increase students' autonomy, engagement, and active learning, as well as contributing to an inclusive learning environment. Technology presents instructors with endless opportunities to optimize these teaching approaches. For example, when adopting the flipped classroom or team-based learning in hybrid courses, instructors can integrate several e-learning at every stage.

"How to Build an Online Learning Community" shares five evidence-based strategies on how to cultivate a social online classroom.

Step 3: Plan for assessment

Assessment is one of the key elements in course design. Therefore, it is important to decide on which assessment types (formative or summative) and specific evaluation criteria to measure whether students meet the learning outcomes. And to facilitate assessment practices that evaluate students fairly and inclusively while contributing to the transfer of lifelong skills, instructors need to use the right assessment tools. Below are some assessment practices and tools to facilitate them:

- Combining self, peer, and teacher assessment

Integrating these three assessment types throughout the course has been proven to help students develop lifelong skills while reducing the workload for teachers. Instructors can effectively exercise this combined approach in hybrid classes with the help of pedagogical technology.

Teachers can rely on different e-learning tools to design projects (portfolios, presentations, videos, etc.) where students submit assignments and then review their peers' work, as well as reflect on their own performance. Finally, instructors provide comments on students' submitted work on the digital platform, identifying misconceptions and providing explanations to help students. Several feedback tools, like peer review, group member evaluation, and assignment review, allow for issuing these feedback types.

- Online discussion and conference

Asynchronous and synchronous discussion is another effective method that instructors can use to establish effective dialogues and communications in online/hybrid settings. The opportunity to provide clear, concise responses to both teachers and peers allows students to cultivate critical thinking and evaluation skills while further reducing teachers' workload.

Pedagogical technology, again, allows teachers to create seamless discussions in online classes. For example, instructors can design discussion group projects, where students work together on a project (a presentation, a video, or a paper), upload their work, then provide feedback on other groups' work based on a given rubric.

- Digital summative assessment

In a face-to-face setting, knowledge-based tests, like quizzes, tests, or exams, are favorite methods to measure students' progress and performance. In the online/blended classrooms however, there are major constraints to how these assessments can be conducted. As students' use of outside resources can't be monitored, knowledge-based tests need to be redesigned to focus on developing higher-order thinking skills and delivering constructive feedback rather than rote memorization. And feedback tools such as quiz and team-based learning, can help you upgrade the traditional pen-and-paper exams.

- Digital performance-based tests

Performance-based strategies, like presentations, videos, or podcasting, are great ways to measure multiple learning objectives and allow students to apply and showcase what they learned. There are plenty of great teaching technologies that allow instructors to replicate on-site performance-based assessments in a blended environment, and feedback tools are among these. Many institutions have used tools such as discussion on work, discussion on topic, assignment and skill review to set up the activities, where learners can present their work and engage in discussion with peers, thus demonstrating their ability to apply knowledge and information learned.

Read more: "4 strategies for effective assessment in online/hybrid learning"

Step 4: Design online/in-person activities and course content

Once the course's goals and assessment have been set, let's decide on the learning activities and resources needed for the course. It is critical to identify activities that capitalize on the advantages of each environment (online and face-to-face). Here are some suggestions of activities suitable for synchronous/asynchronous and in-person sessions, along with the tool suggestions:

Example learning activities and tools

For further suggestions on e-learning tools for hybrid classes, check out this guide: "Designing Hybrid Experiences: Example Learning Activities and Tools."

Developing study content is the most time-consuming aspect of course design. Especially in the online/hybrid settings, instructors need to dedicate certain time deciding on the appropriate types of study materials (written, audio, or video) and the order in which they will go that suits students' learning needs and preferences. Below, you can find suggestions of where to find and craft multimedia course content (click on the image to enlarge):

Step 5: Final touches—ensure for accessibility and interaction

Make sure the course is accessible and inclusive to everyone as your students will be attending the course from different parts of the world, from different platforms (in campus or online) and with time schedules. Also, leave room for online interactions as well since remote teaching makes up for a large part of the course. Instructors can create captions for the video, vary study material types, or combine different teaching approaches to cater for students' diverse needs. Many teaching tools also offer multiple accessibility features, such as automatically generated captions or multimedia file upload.

You can refer to the universal design for learning (UDL) framework or inclusive course design considerations to promote inclusivity and accessibility.

Hybrid learning in action: increasing engagement in a large course

Teachers want to incorporate elements of peer feedback, group work, and automated grading. Feedback peer review was chosen to help instructors reduce the manual workload in grading for this large student cohort while still allowing students to work both individually and in teams to provide meaningful feedback.

The course curriculum is structured with asynchronous lectures in the first half of the week, followed by live sessions in the second half. A peer review assignment was arranged after each live session. For this, students submitted and conducted formative evaluation of each other's submitted executive memo based on a three-criteria rubric designed by teachers in peer review. At the end of the course, they were asked to write a formal memo, which was marked by the instructor as a summative assessment.

SET UP A FUTURE-PROOF
HYBRID CLASSROOM

Tips to set up a future-proof hybrid classroom:

1. Pick up the right hybrid classroom equipment. Consider the needs of your teachers and students.
2. Optimize the delivery of your educational content.
3. Train your teachers and students.
4. Partner with an experienced audio-video solutions company.

A hybrid learning environment blends the best of an in-person and online classroom. You can buy hybrid classroom equipment to set up a one-of-a-kind learning space.

Of course, it pays to plan ahead to get the most value out of your hybrid classroom technology setup. Ultimately, you can hire a hybrid classroom design specialist to create an interactive and engaging learning environment.

Delco Solutions is a top choice for solutions for hybrid learning in Philadelphia and surrounding areas. We can teach you everything you need to know about how to set up a hybrid classroom. Plus, we can help you identify hybrid learning solutions that serve you well, both now and in the future.

Benefits of using a classroom hybrid learning model

- Teachers and students can enjoy the benefits of a hybrid learning model.
- Educators can provide a wide range of digital tools and resources to students. Schools can spend less on the physical space required for in-person learning too.
- Hybrid education gives students greater flexibility. Students can choose a learning style that lines up with their individual needs. They can engage with teachers in person or virtually. This results in personalized learning experiences that a traditional classroom environment cannot match.

Why schools should invest in hybrid education

Hybrid learning became a necessity for schools in the midst of the COVID-19 pandemic. The pandemic has come to an end. However, there is still significant demand for hybrid learning environments globally.

In a 2022 survey of five thousand students and university leaders from around the world, students showed a "clear preference for continuing with at least some online learning," *Forbes* reported. Additionally, 82 percent said they wanted some of their course meetings to take place online, and 41 percent noted they preferred a fully online learning experience.

Hybrid learning will likely play a major role in the future of education. To provide the best possible learning experiences, schools should invest in hybrid education. An audiovisual services company can help your school set up a blended learning environment that benefits your students and teachers long into the future.

HOW TO START A HYBRID LEARNING CENTER

A hybrid learning center can help you maximize simultaneous learning.

As the calendar turns to the 2025 school year, we have to reflect on what did not work with hybrid learning models and instructional practices in our classroom. When we talk about hybrid, we also talk about synchronous, asynchronous, independent learning, and many other terms we never talked about twelve months ago.

The issues we face with hybrid learning is designing lessons that don't fully work for students at home or in the physical classroom. By merging lessons that lack the full range of options in either environment, we have not provided the best learning opportunities to our students.

One promising practice that can be used in hybrid learning is the use of centers. Just like in elementary schools, establishing centers requires some initial planning, work, and possible expense but can save time and money and maximize teacher connections with all learners. Learning centers capitalize on student exploration because they provide students with hands-on experience and teacher support.

Hybrid learning centers

In a hybrid model that makes use of centers, every student attend class synchronously, whether in person or at home. Educators design learning activities that are differentiated for students based on their physical location.

For example, the teacher starts class with a warm-up activity posted on an LMS. Direct instruction via a mini-lesson is provided for all students to access the content together. Centers can then be scheduled in which students engage in either in-person groupings on an LMS or in breakout rooms. The teacher rotates through each group to provide guided practice or support independent work. Once all the centers have been visited, the teacher can provide a closing activity for the whole class, much like the warm-up, in which students reflect on the learning objectives via an online form. Questions can be posted as warm-ups in a way that creates a combined classroom community. Assignments can also be designed with mixed groups in which students at home and in person can collaborate.

While hybrid centers keep students separated based on where they are physically, students still interact through an LMS and synchronous meeting platform. These interactions increase individualized instruction (teachers work directly with all students in each group and ensure they fully understand the content) and student engagement. Centers also allow for an increase and consistency in interactions, much like a full in-person classroom as opposed to traditional A/B hybrid models, in which students are subjected to the delivery of content in person and the completion of individual tasks at home.

ADOPTION OF HYBRID LEARNING CENTERS

Any shifts in current practice takes structured and consistent professional development (PD), training, resources, and time.

Professional development. For districts to launch a consistent instructional practice/model, time and resources will need to be spent to give a clear reason for this shift. This PD will begin with consistent videos around the "why" and the expected outcomes. The message should come from the superintendent and other school leaders.

From there, live PD from in-district or contracted trainers should focus on the implementation of the center model. The agenda will include exemplars, PreK–12, from districts that have successfully implemented this instruction to varying degrees. Additional PD should be added for districts moving away from asynchronous days and to a five-day-a-week synchronous instructional model.

The focus of each session will be on the following:

- Lesson planning
- The technology needed to implement hybrid centers

- Sharing exemplar lessons
- Unit planning
- Detailing support networks

Time. Districts will have to look at the current learning time required to allow for additional days off to implement PD supportive of a significant shift in current practice. Districts can work with school committees/boards to be creative with current vacations and other traditional days off to maximize PD training and time on learning.

Cost. Moving to a fully synchronous model in the hybrid structure will accrue costs to some districts. Initially, the cost of cameras for all teachers in all classrooms will be a requirement. Most laptops have cameras, but some classrooms only have a teacher's desktop. Furthermore, infrastructure in schools will need to be increased—i.e., bandwidth for constant video streaming by all teachers simultaneously. Additional costs for districts could be for families without Internet access. A full synchronous model will also require all students online at home every day during school hours.

Measures of success. A successful PD plan will consist of a solid agenda, highlighting the new model's needs and exemplars. It will also consist of ongoing meetings throughout FY21 to support district implementation. Long-term measures of success will require the collection of data, including but not limited to dropout rates, standardized test scores, and district common assessments, as each pertains to the FY21 school year and beyond.

Learning is dynamic and complicated, and teaching in a hybrid model adds another layer of complexity. However, by being intentional, consistent, and routinized via synchronous hybrid models, we can create a learning environment more closely resembling that which existed pre-COVID and in the best interest of our learners.

IN-CLASS HYBRID LEARNING SOLUTIONS

This is a solution for premium hybrid education for audiovisual teaching in all countries. Our team can help you set up a hybrid learning environment that performs as expected and won't break your budget. Some students learn best when they're interacting with their peers. Those that take hybrid courses may find that their fellow students just don't post as often or participate as much as they'd like, just doing enough to meet the minimum requirements and pass the class.

What are disadvantages of hybrid learning?

How does hybrid schooling work?

Hybrid schools utilize a combination of at-school and at-home learning, but there can be much variety in how they are structured. Students may meet in person two days and learn at home three days, or the other way around. Some hybrids meet half days in person, while the rest of the time is spent at home.

WHAT IS HYBRID CLASS, AND HOW DOES IT WORK?

Types of hybrid classes:

Depending on the institution, the hybrid class offerings may vary. Here's a look at some of the different types of formats:

- Face-to-face driver: During face-to-face learning time, instructors lecture and allow for questions. Based on what is taught in class, online assignments and homework are administered.
- Online driver: For online driver hybrid classes, the lectures take place online via streaming. There may also be a requirement for students to take part in forums and discussions online. For the time spent in class, students can ask questions, talk to their peers, and receive one-on-one aid.
- Days in / days out: Days in and days out is more typically deployed in K–12 settings as opposed to college. It rose in popularity during the COVID-19 pandemic and consists of some days in the

classroom learning (two to three per week), and the other days are spent learning online.

- Lab rotation: For subjects that require hands-on experience, lectures take place online, and the in-person portion is for the lab work.
- Flex: Flex hybrid classes mix both learning styles in sections. For example, for the first quarter or half of a semester, students may learn online. Then the setup switches to fully in-person classes.

Pros of hybrid classes

When hybrid classes are well structured, and both students and professors are all-in, then there are many benefits to be had from this type of learning.

Check out this abbreviated list of pros:

On-demand lectures. When lectures are streamed or recorded, students may have the option to log on and learn whenever their schedule permits. This type of flexibility is really helpful for many students, especially those who have other responsibilities to maintain while learning.

To exemplify, students who work or have families to raise may have more restrictive schedules and would otherwise be unable to attend lectures at 9:00 a.m., Monday through Friday. With some instruction online, they don't have to sacrifice and miss important lectures.

Effective in-person time. When students are in classrooms every day, they may take face time for granted. When there's a limited amount of time to spend in front of a professor or fellow peers, then the time may be spent more effectively.

Learning styles. Different students have different learning styles. For some, the in-person and traditional way of learning is well suited. For others, online and digital learning when the lecture can be paused, rewound, or replayed can help them absorb material better. A hybrid class can optimize the way certain students learn.

Maximize time. With blended courses, students can maximize their time and have more control over the pace at which they move through material. Students have the option to post questions in forums and work with peers online or in person.

When students do meet in the classroom, they will likely be more prepared to ask the questions they still need to address. If they have understood material from a lecture that's recorded, they are able to allocate their time to the aspects of the lecture that they still need to work on grasping.

Cost-effective. Hybrid classes cost less than traditional in-person college courses. For starters, there's no need to commute daily, which can drive up transportation and gas costs. The commute also poses an opportunity cost that can pull students away from time working or being with their family. Additionally, hybrid classes may cost less per unit because there's less time spent on campus.

Things to consider before taking a hybrid class

Some inflexibility. When compared to traditional classes, hybrid classes are more flexible. However, when compared to fully online classes, there exists some inflexibility in terms of the in-person learning sessions. These are often mandatory. So when signing up for hybrid classes, you still have to make sure that the time spent in the classroom fits within your schedule.

Commitment. As with any type of education, there's commitment required. When you enroll in a hybrid class, you have to manage your own time, especially when it comes to the online portion.

Difference between hybrid class and online class

The main difference between a hybrid and online class is that online classes are 100 percent online. Hybrid classes bring in the component of in-person learning, no matter how large or small that portion of the hybrid class will be.

Online classes offer the most flexibility of any type of education. That being said, some learners still like to have that face-to-face aspect, in which case, the hybrid model may offer the perfect solution.

Fully online options

If you're leaning more toward the fully online option, then University of the People has you covered! We offer fully online degree programs in four disciplines: health science, education, business administration, and computer science. These degrees are some of the most sought-after and highly in demand in the world.

Along with the immensely flexible and accessible online classroom, every program is also tuition-free! Once you graduate from University of the People, your accredited degree will open the door to endless career opportunities.

A mixed learning experience

The options for obtaining your degree these days are more wide-ranging than ever before. You have the choice to choose between on-campus classes, online classes, or a hybrid class, which mixes both. Depending on your personal desires, schedule, budget, location, and the like, you can assess which learning setup is best for you.

Discover what's trending with our popular content. Explore here: "13 Inspiring Educational Quotes for Students."

Throughout your educational journey, it's likely that you'll look for sources of motivation since you'll be tasked with a lot and will have your fair share of response.

STRUCTURE OF A MINISTRY

Various denominations have deacons, archdeacons, evangelists, apostles, prophets, pastors, senior pastors, elders, overseers, bishops.

If you're unaware of how to make your church grow, maybe you should consider looking into church leadership structure models. It's not easy to alter a leadership structure, but it's necessary in order to accommodate the growth of the church.

Growing a church takes more than prayer and preaching to the choir. One of the main barriers to growth in a church is its structure. What leads to success in growing a church is coming up with a well-maintained church organizational structure. A leader must also pursue with passion and build a vibrant community. Part of the structure you can't forget about creating is a church administration structure that works seamlessly, keeping members informed and engaged with tools like a church financial report. A non-profit church must keep accurate financial information to maintain 501C3 status. These financial statements may not be needed for tax filings, but they are still incredibly important to describe the church's finances, which helps manage a church's finances and budget.

Church leadership structure

Discover church leadership structure models that churches can use to organizational structures for church growth.

A pastor is the leader of a church. The title *pastor* also refers to specific roles within a church. These roles typically include preaching and teaching during worship services, discipling believers one-on-one or in small groups, providing counseling.

Elder. An elder is a church leader who serves within the church and community. They are to look out for the spiritual of God's people, and they do so by leading by exam.

Additionally, they should be people of prayer and study understand how to guide others.

The bishop supports the work of local pastors and congregations through their travels from church to church.

When it comes to leading within the church, understanding leadership roles and church administration structures is not something you should take lightly. There are many different leadership roles in the church, but each plays an integral part in what makes a church successful.

Pastor. A pastor is the leader of a church. The title *pastor* also refers to specific roles within a church. These roles typically include:

- Preaching and teaching during worship services
- Discipling believers one-on-one or in small groups
- Providing counseling

Other duties of the pastor include administrative tasks, such as planning events and activities for church members to participate in outside of worship service times. In most cases, pastors get help from other pastors, elders, and deacons to help carry out the responsibilities of shepherding God's people.

Bishop. Bishops are the highest level of leadership in many churches and are important to consider in your church leadership structure models. They have authority over a group of churches and are often called overseers or superintendents. A bishop must also maintain proper doctrinal interpretation within each parish under their jurisdiction.

As such, bishops are not responsible for day-to-day decision-making. Instead, they support the work of local pastors and congregations through their travels from church to church.

In the church, bishops help keep things running smoothly and make decisions about things, like preaching, giving out the sacraments, ensuring that people have faith and morals, and teaching them about religion.

While their roles may sound similar to a pastor's, bishops are leaders of the Christian clergy, while pastors are the ordained leaders of the Christian congregation.

Elder. An elder is a church leader who serves within the church and its community. But what does that mean? According to 1 Peter 5:1–4, elders are godly men of character who shepherd the people in their care.

They are to look out for the spiritual health of God's people, and they do so by leading by example. For instance, elders should be above reproach because they are well-respected in their communities (1 Timothy 3:2).

Additionally, they should be men of prayer and Scripture study to help them understand how to guide others.

The responsibilities of elders vary depending on the size and needs of each church. For example, some churches see their elders as primarily responsible for teaching and preaching from Scripture. However, the preaching may fall on pastors or deacons in other churches, yet most churches have elders who serve on committees that deal with budgeting or outreach.

Minister. A minister has many different meanings in Christianity, but essentially it describes anyone who acts in service to others through prayer or by teaching about their faith. Ministers can be either male or female, even children.

Ordained ministers are clergies who serve as leaders within their respective churches. Ministers can also be bishops and elders, should their church choose to ordain them.

Associate pastor. An associate pastor is a minister who works under a senior pastor. The term *associate pastor* is typically used to describe an ordained minister who serves in a church's executive or assistant leadership position. An associate pastor may take on many different roles within the church, including youth ministry, administrative, and outreach.

Deacon. Deacons are responsible for assisting the pastor and elders in leading the congregation. This includes tasks such as

- caring for community members who are sick,
- welcoming visitors,
- serving communion,
- working with the youth.

They should be good role models for others in the church, setting a high example of what it means to walk in faith.

Health maintenance organization (HMO)

Does a church itself require health maintenance organization (HMO) coverage? HMOs are health insurance plans designed to provide health care services to individuals or groups of individuals. They are usually offered by employers or purchased by individuals to cover their health care needs.

However, churches may choose to offer health insurance coverage to their employees, including pastors, clergy members, or staff members. In such cases, the church could opt for an HMO plan as part of its employee benefits package. This would provide health care coverage to eligible employees and their dependents within the network of health care providers affiliated with the HMO.

It's worth noting that the decision to offer health insurance, including HMO plans, is dependent on the church's policies, budget, and the size of the organization. Churches are not obligated to provide health insurance, but many choose to do so as a way to support their employees and their well-being.

Understanding church finances is essential to maintaining the overall health of any church. A leadership team's ability to fulfill their mission is deeply connected to how well they steward resources and manage their church's funds. When done correctly, churches can use their finances to reach more people, make more disciples, and have a greater impact on their communities!

Let's take a look at ten simple church accounting practices that will help you learn the basics of how to manage church finances while also promoting biblical stewardship among your team.

1. Calculate your church's expenses

One of the first steps for managing your church's finances is to map out your current expenses. As Benjamin Franklin wisely said, "Beware of little expenses. A small leak will sink a great ship."

With the help of your church's financial software, start by listing out all of your operating expenses. These include items such as the following:

- *Personnel*—salaries, payroll taxes, benefits, insurance
- *Facilities*—rent or mortgage, maintenance, utilities
- *Administrative*—office supplies, Internet, taxes
- *Engagement tools*—church website, custom mobile app, live streaming
- *Ministry and outreach*—missions, youth/children ministries, evangelism

2. Track current income

The donations, gifts, and any other contributions that your church receives make up the annual income. Most income comes from donations in the form of cash, checks, and online giving. Other donations to track include fund-raising campaigns, stocks, securities, and noncash contributions, such as household items, vehicles, boats, etc.

Fortunately, the trend of accepting online donations and using church accounting software has streamlined the process for keeping tabs on your church's income! The best online giving solutions, such as Subsplash Giving, will automatically record your incoming donations for you and allow you to easily generate giving reports. They will also allow you to accept and track payments for noncharitable transactions, such as event tickets or merchandise.

3. Forecast future income

Based on your historical expenses and contributions, you can begin the process of forecasting your church's future income. When making your projection, pay close attention to patterns in your attendance and giving.

A good financial practice is to err on the side of caution when projecting income. Be realistic with your estimates. You should also encourage your donors to set up recurring gifts through your online giving provider. This allows them to schedule their regular tithes and offerings, giving your church access to more accurate data about future income!

4.   Create a yearly church budget

Your church budget should be based on your church's expenses and projected income, but it should also be driven by your vision and goals. Use your income forecast as the base to allocate funds to different ministries to reach their individual and collective goals.

One place to start is asking each ministry department leader—like your missions director or youth pastor—to submit their own department budget based on their goals, needs, and resources. It's important not to assume that your staff and other leaders understand how to create budgets, so provide financial training for your team! Doing this allows your leadership team to take ownership of their budget and better understand the impact of their financial decisions, rather than just simply administering a handed-down budget.

5.   Offer an online giving solution

If your church doesn't already offer online giving, now is the perfect time to start! Studies show that adding an online giving solution dramatically increases overall giving by an average of 32 percent! Donors appreciate the convenience and security of online giving through their mobile church app or website, as well as text-to-give. They can also easily view their online donations and download their end-of-year giving statements.

For your church finance team, online giving simplifies administrative tasks, such as sending out giving statements or pulling financial reports. It also helps your church anticipate future donations through regular recurring giving.

6. Set aside a three- to six-month emergency fund

We can always expect to be faced with the unexpected. Despite all of the budgeting and planning, unanticipated expenses occur each and every year. This is why finance experts suggest creating an emergency fund equal to three to six months of typical expenses. You'll also want to clearly define what kind of situation constitutes an emergency in order to protect this cash reserve from being used for nonemergency purposes. When not fully used, this reserve fund can increase annually and will help protect your church from budget shortfalls.

7. Establish an oversight policy for managing church finances

A church's financial committee is usually made up of members who were assigned or elected to steward the church's financial resources. They're responsible for ensuring that the church's finances are being handled responsibly, ethically, and in alignment with the church's vision.

Part of this responsibility should include creating a written oversight policy that includes the following:

- A code of ethics and conduct that each person handling church funds must sign and agree to.

- A schedule for regularly pulling financial reports and monitoring financial activities.
- A list of the duties of a treasurer in a church for sharing financial reports.
- A team—not just one person—that is responsible for reviewing everything regarding church money.
- A cash-handling policy for counting and depositing cash and checks. This should include rotating teams and regular reviews for irregularities.
- A schedule for an external audit of the church's finances once a year by an independent third party. This is a safety measure. Compare their findings with your church's internal finance reports.
- A process for reporting suspicious financial activities or potential fraud.

8. Review financial reporting

Being good stewards of your church's finances requires creating regular church financial reports for the finance committee. These reports should be presented each quarter and should be written in a way that is easily understood. Church leaders should also have access to review these reports and ask questions if something seems amiss.

An incredible 80 percent of church fraud cases go unreported every year! Financial reports and reviews are key safeguards against theft, fraud, and embezzlement. Any concerns that are raised should enact oversight policy procedures to ensure accuracy and accountability.

9. Set up a church debt management strategy

Many churches take on debt throughout their lifetimes for a variety of reasons: to help when getting started, to allow them to grow and expand, or simply in order to keep the church open and operating. But long-term or growing debt can cripple a church's ability to effectively reach their goals.

This is why it's important to have a strategy for paying down church debt. This should include dedicating a portion of the annual budget to debt reduction, as well as planning capital campaigns. Being debt-free will allow the church to explore new growth opportunities and increase their ability to impact their communities in positive and practical ways!

10. Share your church financial statements and vision with your congregation

Today's church donors expect transparency and accountability; they appreciate understanding how their contributions are impacting their communities. At the end of each calendar year, hold a meeting with your congregation to

- revisit your vision and financial goals that were set for the year,
- review your church financial statements,
- share stories that celebrate the accomplishments made possible by their donations.

Talking about money and finances is not always easy to do, but the reality is that your church's finances are a critical part of being able to complete your unique mission. Understanding where your church is financially, sharing your goals, making safety protocols, offering tools that streamline giving, and sharing your accomplishments will all go a long way in encouraging donors to give even more willingly to your church!

GET THE CHURCH BUDGETING GUIDE!

The church finance best practices covered in this article are just the tip of the iceberg! To get even more advice on how to be a good steward of your church's resources, download your free copy of the "Church Budgeting Guide" today. This free twenty-seven-page guide contains all of this and much more:

- Church budget templates
- Step-by-step budget creation guide
- Top budgeting tips from real pastors
- How to avoid church financial disasters

Nonprofit status for religious organizations

Churches, synagogues, mosques, and other places of worship are automatically considered tax-exempt by the IRS (as long as they meet certain requirements), without filing for recognition of 501(c)(3) status officially. So why would a church file for 501(c)(3) status? Let's delve into the legal requirements to be considered automatically tax-exempt and why a place of worship might choose to file for 501c3 status with the IRS. We'll use the word *church* throughout this article, but this applies to places of worship of all religions.

What is legally required to be considered a church (or place of worship) with the IRS?

The IRS has a formal list of attributes associated with churches, but let's break down those requirements. Churches need to have distinct legal existence, which simply means, the church needs to be incorporated as an entity with your state. If you'd like assistance incorporating your church with your state, please contact us and we can help. We've helped religious organizations get started all over the country.

The IRS also describes having a form of worship and/or creed, literature, regular religious services, and an established place of worship. For most churches, this simply means that there is an established way to practice your religion, whether you have a religious text (like the Torah), a building or place outside that your worship or church services are held, and some form of written explanation as to what your belief system entails. The IRS lists fifteen attributes. Your place of worship does not need to meet all fifteen in order to be considered a church. They look at the combination of attributes your organization possesses and determine from there if the organization will legally be considered a church or not.

You might be surprised; many organizations that we don't traditionally or colloquially consider to be a church are in fact recognized by the IRS as churches. This means they get all the benefits—less oversight, non-filing of 990s, etc.

Why would a church file for 501(c)(3) tax-exempt status if they aren't required to?

It's common for churches to still apply for 501(c)(3) status, even though they aren't legally required to do so. There are a few reasons for this:

1. Having 501(c)(3) status assures your congregation and donors that the church is recognized officially by the IRS as legitimate and tax-exempt, thus guaranteeing their donations and tithes will be tax deductible.

2. 501(c)(3) status increases the transparency of the organization, as the church will then be required to file a tax return (called IRS form 990) each year. Those forms are available to the public, again ensuring donors know that their money is being used in a charitable way. For churches who provide programming, like missions work or children's programs, this transparency can be a great way to let donors know that their contributions are going to a worthy cause.

3. Another factor is that 501(c)(3) organizations are given a variety of discounts and benefits. Many companies have programs that discount their services or products for established nonprofits like churches but require 501(c)(3) status to ensure the legitimacy of the organization. The US Postal Service also offers discounted rates for mailing and postage for established 501(c)(3) organizations.

4. Some states provide additional tax exemptions for established 501(c)(3) organizations, like exemption from state sales tax or state employment tax. These tax exemptions can help churches spend more of their funding on their religious services and programs. Rather than pay taxes all churches should be registered 501C3's.

Not all churches in the US are registered 501(c)(3) organizations, but it could be right for your church.

Five things to consider when determining a pastor's salary

Financial pressure is one of the main sources of stress among pastors. In this article, we will explore how much you should pay your pastor and some of the guidelines you can use to do it well. This may not eliminate all the financial stress your pastor faces, but it can ensure your church is doing everything they can to help.

I am explaining how you pay your pastor is a gospel issue that has impact on the effectiveness of your church and its mission. A church that is not obedient to God cannot expect God's blessing on their mission. So each church, no matter its size, should do everything in their power to ensure that their pastor is fully supplied (Philippians 4:18). Their pastor should see that they are being generous (Galatians 6:6–8) and not stingy. A church that is cheap with their pastor will suffer the consequences. The pastor will see that he is being treated with contempt and that the church is not properly honoring God. It's hard to minister in this context without becoming resentful. Here are five things to consider as you plan your pastor's salary.

1. What is the size of the congregation?

The size of a congregation will be the greatest determining factor for the church's budget. Large congregations with multiple staff can afford to pay pastors better than a church of forty that is struggling to survive. Because these worlds are so vastly different, we will focus on the larger group: the small church. Ninety percent of churches in the United States have less than 350 people attend each week; 64 percent have less than 200. The average church size in America is 89 adults. Thom Rainer says that it takes a ratio of 76:1—meaning, an average weekly attendance of 76 is the minimum needed to pay one full-time staff member. If these numbers are correct, then a large percentage of American churches will struggle to pay a full-time pastor. So how does a small church determine how much to pay their pastor?

2. What percentage of the budget will be allocated to staff salary?

Small-church expert, Karl Vaters, says, "While 45 to 55 percent of budget going to staff is healthy for mid-size to larger churches, the range is much wider for small churches, as in zero to 100 percent." When we take church size into account, it makes sense that smaller churches will have to spend a larger portion of their budget to pay a full-time pastor. According to the Evangelical Covenant Church, a healthy congregation with a weekly average attendance of 150 people should spend 40 to 50 percent of their total budget on staff salary. If, however, the church only has forty people, they will probably need to spend 55 to 65 percent of their total budget; anything above 60 percent is very risky.

Thom Rainer says that the average staffing costs among all churches has dropped from 54 percent to 49 percent in recent years. Church consultant, Tony Morgan, says, "Our consulting team generally encourages churches to try to stay in the range of 45 to 55 percent of total budget." So what percentage of your total budget should your church spend on staff salary? Whatever amount you determine is generous but not too risky.

3. Is this a livable wage?

When you have determined the percentage of your budget available for the pastor's pay, you will be able to tell if you can afford a full-time pastor or not. The living wage calculator will help you determine what hourly wage your pastor will need to live in your state and county based on his family size and how many people in the family are working. Use that number to determine a yearly salary; this amount should be the minimum your church will pay (if possible). Remember, this living wage calculator does not include benefits (more on that later).

Now factor in the unique housing situation of your church. Does the church own a parsonage? If so, this will allow you to reduce the percentage of your budget dedicated to staff pay. However, be sure you have budgeted for the upkeep of the building and the tax implications for the pastor. If your pastor has to buy or rent his home, then he qualifies for a ministerial housing allowance. This means that the church can designate a portion of his salary as housing allowance, and whatever he uses as qualified housing expenses will be tax-free. This amount can be whatever percentage of his total salary he will use, but it may be wise to keep it under 50 percent to avoid an audit by the IRS. I do not recommend lowering the amount of pay because of a housing allowance. This tax benefit for pastors is being challenged in the courts, and churches may be forced to rethink their budgets in the near future.

4.   Does this budget leave room for inflation?

One of the most overlooked parts of budgeting for a pastor's pay is the cost of inflation. Fewer than 60 percent of churches give their pastor a cost of living increase each year. Inflation rises between 1 and 4 percent every year; it rarely goes down (that would be deflation). In order to maintain the value of your pastor's salary, you need to raise it with inflation every year. Otherwise, you will be asking your pastor to live on less value. Consider this example:

A church pays their pastor a salary of $34,000 in 2000. The consumer price index for the Midwest region in January 2000 was almost 165. In January 2019, it was almost 234. That means, in 2019, the pastor's salary should be just over $48,000 to have equal value.

($34,000 x 234) / 165 = $48,218

This means that if the church didn't keep up with inflation, the pastor's salary would have almost $14,000 less in perceived value. What was a livable wage becoming substandard over time. This example is just an illustration, of course; there are more factors to consider (local economy, housing market, etc.).

5. How much will be allocated toward benefits?

Most denominations recommend that benefits be calculated separately from salary. Do not calculate a living wage and reduce it by taking the cost of benefits from that amount. Most churches who can afford to pay benefits offer health insurance and/or retirement. Check with your denomination about the plans that they offer. My denomination offers a pension plan that performs very well compared to most, but it requires that the church contribute a minimum of 6 percent of the pastor's total salary. As a general rule in 2019, most churches should plan on between $10,000 and $20,000 in benefits expenses per employee (remember, that's on top of salary). This is out of reach for many small churches. In this case, they would do better to raise the pastor's salary rather than paying for benefits that are not much benefit.

When these five factors are considered, the church will have a good picture of what it can pay. For most small churches, this means they will not be able to pay their pastor the double honor that he may deserve (1 Timothy 5:17–18).

What if we can't afford to pay a pastor enough to fully supply his needs?

If a church can't afford to pay a full-time pastor's salary and benefits, they may consider some creative options. These options are less than ideal and may affect the church's ability to fulfill its mission. They require making some hard choices and asking the pastor to make serious sacrifices. Additionally, not all pastors have a personality that will work with these options. If your church has to choose one of these options, make sure you honor your pastor in many other ways.

Ask your pastor to raise his own support.

Both Jesus and Paul had ministries that were supported by others (Luke 8:2–3; Philippians 4:18). *The God Ask* is a great resource for how to make this work in today's culture. Please recognize that if your pastor has to raise his own support; this will take a substantial amount of time every week. This time should be considered part of his work for the church, not something he should do in his spare time. I have heard of churches that expect a pastor to raise his own financial support from both within and outside the congregation. They offer no guaranteed salary, but the people of the church give toward his financial needs. In one church, they placed a black box at the back of the sanctuary, and the pastor had the only key. No one knew how much the pastor received.

Invocational ministry

Acts 18:3 describes Paul as a tentmaker, so it seems some of his income came from working in the marketplace. Today, tentmaking is often used to describe someone who gets all their income from a marketplace job so they can minister at no cost to the church. Whether all or part of his income must come from another job, the vocational pastor will need the congregation to fill in some gaps. He simply cannot do everything a full-time pastor can do. Additionally, many vocational pastors have two part-time jobs that offer no benefits and no vacation. The church would be wise to find ways to give their pastor extra time off, maybe even take up a special collection or raise funds to send the pastor and his family on a vacation every year. Every vocational pastor that I know is seriously overworked. If your pastor is invocational, be sure he is getting Sabbath rest and time alone with God for his own spiritual nourishment. If not, your church is likely doing damage to your pastor and his family. Many vocational pastors would disagree with me, but I've seen too many burn out to believe this is healthy.

Join with another church

Many churches today are merging with another church in their area so that the combined congregation can support a full-time pastor. In some cases, this is one church with two separate memberships because they represent two denominations under one roof. Other churches have become satellite campuses of a larger church. This allows the pastor to do the preaching and shepherding of the campus church while much of the administration and programs are handled by the large church. It can be a great partnership when carefully planned.

What are some ways we can honor our pastor that won't cost the church much?

- *Encourage the congregation to give the pastor gifts* (gift cards, produce from their garden, a used car that's still in good condition, use of a family cabin, etc.).
- *Give your pastor extra vacation time.* I believe a pastor should have a minimum of four weeks of vacation and two to four weeks of study leave. Pulpit supply is cheaper than finding a new pastor. A burned-out pastor will cost the church far more than paid time off.
- *Send your pastor on a retreat.* There are many free or low-cost options for pastors and their families. Do some research, and find one that will work. Be sure to give them something for food and gas if they aren't paid well.

HE CALLED, I ANSWERED

You Called!

He called;
I did not answer the phone.
He called and left a message. I heard his
    voice and erased it.
I took the phone off of the hook; he got a
    busy signal.
He came to my house, knocked on my
    door;
I hid behind the curtain.
When I was in bed,
I could hear his voice.
I was afraid to shut my eyes.
Finally, when I least expected it, on a
    Sunday night,
When I was with friends,
He called.
I had no place to hide.
A cold chill passed through my body;
    sweat broke out on my forehead. He
    called. I listen.

He said, "This is God. I need you!"
"Lord," I answered,
"I am not ready. I am afraid.
Please call on someone else
To do your work.
I do not have the knowledge
To bring even myself back to you, let alone
    one of your lost sheep." He called. I
    listen.
"Anything you need, I will provide you,"
Said the Lord,
"Any words that need to be written, I will
    guide you," said the Lord. "My child,
    I have been training you for many
    years, and now you are ready.
Take my staff.
It is time I stopped carrying you, and it is
    time for you to take my word to my
    children." He called. I listen.
And now His words are written by me!
When I *was* called, I answered, "Yes, Lord,
    here I am!"

One of the many issues I faced when called to ministry in 1999 was the understanding of the Trinity.

After studying the Bible, reading, and writing year after year, I could not correlate in my mind how God the Father, the Son, and the Holy Ghost could be the same God!

God waited one year before he revealed this knowledge to me.

There are three incidents as described how God confirmed that the Trinity is but one God.

First, as we know God thinks it.

Second, we know the Word speaks it.

Third, we know the Holy Ghost does it.

In this relationship, God reveals to me that

- our mind thinks it,
- our mouth speaks it,
- our hands do it.

If in fact we are one with our thoughts and our words, why cannot God then do the same thing? Why cannot God think it, speak it, and do it through His thoughts, His words, and His actions?

However, our minds need something material. We need something physical to understand. So God says, "I want you to take a three-bladed fan and write on the blades of the fan in three different colors—the Father, the Son and the Holy Ghost."

God chose the three colors to be blue, red, and white.

So I took the blades of the fan and painted them, the Father, the Son, and the Holy Ghost, using the three colors God gave me, and I turned the fan on.

The revelation was I could no longer see the Father, the Son, and the Holy Ghost. The three colors became the color purple, which is God's color, and the wind from the fan became the breath of the words of our Father as described throughout the Bible, including Moses in the book of Genesis.

Until today I was unable to remember the three colors God gave me. As it came to my mind, I concluded red, white, and blue means the color of God.

What other symbol do we have that is red, white, and blue?

What do the three colors stand for?

Well, to begin with, we know red is the blood of Jesus, and we know white is purity, and we also know the blue symbolizes the heavens and the waters, which God covers us with.

But even greater is the symbol of the American flag.

The American flag stands for the blood that we spilled. The white is the purity of our hearts and our country, and the blue is the air and the purity of our waters, which makes up 70 percent of our body.

"About 71 percent of the Earth's surface is water covered, and the oceans hold about 96.5 percent of all Earth's water."

Then God gave me the third insight; the understanding where Jesus was baptized, and God was in the heavens, and He looked down upon His Son and said, "This is My beloved Son in whom I Am well pleased."

This created a new issue. Why would God look down upon a part of Him that was not Himself but the Son, and say, "this is My beloved Son in whom I Am well pleased"?

God revealed this to me: Do we not have thoughts?

Do we not speak to ourselves? And do we not answer ourselves?

Why then should God, as the Trinity, be limited to not being able to do this as well?

So when God spoke from the heavens, "This is My Son," He was speaking to Himself, and He was in fact saying, I am pleased with what I am doing.

So anytime you have a conversation with yourself, know you're doing something that is no different than what God does. We have the power of thoughts, we have the power of our words, and we have the power of our deeds to do God's work every day.

I just received a word from God—simple: "a new beginning."

Go figure.

> For I know the plans I have for you, declares the Lord, plans for welfare and not for evil, to give you a future and a hope. (Jeremiah 29:11)

> Behold, I am doing a new thing; now it springs forth, do you not perceive it? I will make a way in the wilderness and rivers in the desert. (Isaiah 43:19)

> Ask, and it will be given to you; seek, and you will find; knock, and it will be opened to you. (Matthew 7:7)

> If my people who are called by my name humble themselves and pray and seek my face and turn from their wicked ways, then I will hear from heaven and

will forgive their sin and heal their land. (2 Chronicles 7:14)

And he who was seated on the throne said, "Behold, I am making all things new." Also, he said, "Write this down, for these words are trustworthy and true." (Revelation 21:5)

RESUME AND INFORMATION CONCERNING THE AUTHOR

Apostle Charles Frederick Tolbert DivM, EdM, EdD, PhD

- Retired US Army
- Bachelor's degree in organizational effectiveness (BS)—University of Maryland
- Master of theology (DivM)—Logos University
- Master of education and technology (EdM)—AIU
- Doctor in educational leadership (EdD)—NSU
- Doctor of philosophy/theology/education (PhD)—AIDANU

Apostle Charles Frederick Tolbert is currently teaching internationally with the long-term goal of establishing virtual reality hybrid school systems.

Systematic theology is a discipline of Christian theology that formulates an orderly, rational, and coherent account of the doctrines of the Christian faith. It addresses issues such as what the Bible teaches about certain topics or what is true about God and his universe.

Dr. Tolbert's intention is to bring ministries into a global virtual reality hybrid school/university system, where there is homeschooling, teaching in the assembly, and combining it in the classrooms with on-the-job training. Walking Your Vision University teaching is systematic theology.

There are 195 countries that he intends to expand the training within five to ten years (www.calltoduty.org).

> Behold, I will send my messenger, and he shall prepare the way before me: and the LORD, whom ye seek, shall suddenly come to his temple, even the messenger of the covenant, whom ye delight in: behold, he shall come, saith the LORD of hosts. (Malachi 3:1)

Education:

Doctoral degree in theology philosophy, PhD—AIDANU–Jacksonville, Florida

- + Doctoral degree in educational leadership—Nova Southeastern University, May 2010, Ft. Lauderdale, Florida
- + Masters in theology, Graduate School, Jacksonville, Florida.
- + Masters of education in information technology, American Intercontinental University–Ft. Lauderdale, Florida.

+ Ordained CFACS, Inc.—upon completion of one year of teaching from CFACS, Inc. Academy–Ft. Lauderdale, Florida (http//<u>www.cfacs.com</u>)

+ Ordained New Generation Ministries, Inc.—completion of one year of teaching, Ft. Lauderdale, Florida.

+ University of Kingdom Living graduate, licensed minister

+ Bachelor of science in business management—University of Maryland–College Park, Maryland

+ Graduate work course in organizational effectiveness and performance appraisal—University of Maryland–College Park, Maryland

+ Administrative training workshop—Cindy Trimm Ministry by Dr. Trimm

+ Completed the new membership classes of Embassy Worship Center

+ Attended over twenty Monday night–leadership classes by EWC

+ Worked with the Catholic Church and received training in marriage encounter

+ Deacon, outreach program—Solid Rock

+ Prison minister 2001 and other committee memberships for Summit Impact 1999 and 2000 for EWC

+ Debbie Leakey's Ministry, helping young women

+ Security team for EWC

+ Various committees to assist elderly in the Catholic Church

+ Various committees for the Special Olympics

^ Author: See website for my books and teachings: http://www.cfacs.com
* Twenty-two years of military schools and leadership position—retired master sergeant
* Strong leadership, organizational skills, orator, strong written and interpersonal communication skills; familiarity with all aspects of the organization of a church and know how to present God's word; ability to acquire and present detailed information and to establish rapport with a wide variety of people; ideally suited to accomplish any task given

Employment history:

* October 2005–Present: Founder of Citizens for a Better America, Inc.
* October 1999–Present: Studying the works of Christ Jesus, ordained minister, president and founder of Christ Found All Creation Saved (CFACS, Inc.), a nonprofit organization dedicated to bringing men home through men's awareness programs
* August 1994–October 1999: President/sole proprietor and oversight, entire company operation. Owning this aircraft sales company provided a better understanding of problems by business owners and major corporations; bought and sold 175 aircraft.
* June 1982–August 1994: Independent contractor: Aircraft Sales—in charge of all aspects of aircraft sales company, Bought and sold over forty-four aircraft (director of sales). My responsibilities included but

were not limited to coordinating administrative and sales functions; brokering executive aircraft, including turbo props and jet aircraft; making all decisions affecting budget, contracting, and marketing; locating buyers and sellers, building financial packages, and acquiring and maintaining exclusive listings; working with financial and leasing companies; and providing operation leases for South America.

* June 1981–July 1982: Success Motivation International, Annapolis, Maryland distributor/sole proprietor. Responsibilities included all aspects of marketing motivation and material designed to increase individual and company sales, conducting lectures, workshops, and seminars.

* April 1960–May 1981: United States Army retired master sergeant, twenty-two years of active duty; last assignment as operational director, US Communications Command Washington, DC; Directing personnel in telecommunication centers; plans officer; platoon sergeant; instructor for junior noncommission officers, writing the training guide to be used for these soldiers at Ft. Gordon Georgia; served in Vietnam.

* Five Bronze Stars
* Two Meritorious Service Medals
* Three Army Commendation Medals
* Six Good Conduct Medals
* National Defense Services Medal
* Four Vietnam Service Medals
* Republic of Vietnam Campaign Ribbon 1960

* Expert Badge with rifle bar
* Advanced leadership and counseling schools with the US Army Services
* The first member of the Sergeant Morales Club, March 1974

Thank you for your reading and responding to the book systematic theology through the spiritual eye.

APPENDIX 1

Charles Tolbert <cfabamerica@gmail.com>
to me
Ethical Dilemma in Modern Society
Charles Frederick Tolbert, EdD
CFABA
Citizens for a Better America
cfabamerica@gmail.com, www.cfabamerica.com
Written by Charles F. Tolbert, PhD, EdD, EdM, DivM, BS, and retired master sergeant

Introduction:

The purpose of this article is to pinpoint the improper behavior of Acts to Resolve Legal Conflict in any behavior by a politician, educator, or human resource department (HRD) that would cause conflict with the codes of ethics as outlined by American Psychology Association (APA, 2009) and increase public trust. Should the counselor's ethical responsibility conflict with the law, they should resolve the conflict in a professional manner.

When an ethical standard is bridged, it has to be identified as a violation and brought to the attention of an ethics committee to determine the legality of the enforcement of the conflict entrusted between the public servant and the general public. If there is no immediate harm to either, parts of the general population and this procedure does not violate ethical standards, determination on how to resolve the matter can be reviewed through legal counseling. Unfortunately, there can be a conflict which would not allow the client to fully disclose his or her emotional state.

The behavior which violates a chosen ethical standard when there is a legal conflict can be a line finely drawn. Many HRDs are torn between ethical credibility and communication with their client and the legal consequences. The general practices outlined in the code of conduct for psychologist under APA establishes standard, which should be adhered to and summarizes the intent of APA. By notifying the client at the beginning of the session and getting a written consent by the client that any information discussed, which breaks any legal law or moral standard has to be reported, is the first step of avoiding conflict with the client and the legality of the law. The conflict of ethics and law changes dramatically, noted by Ivey, Ivey, and Zalaquett, 2010, when dealing outside the continental United States, may be legally correct in one country but varies drastically in other countries.

One of the issues we have in society today is, what is the responsibility of the HRD to society, and how is this society defined? If you were to pinpoint the improper behavior, you would find the ethical principle of social responsibility (Gobodo-Madikizela, 2008). Social responsibility extends beyond day-to-day work for the HRD. The humanitarian responsibilities should be reviewed as a primary task of social responsibility. Gobodo-Madikizela (2008) wrote his articles to address the violence in Africa and how foreigners were affected by this violence. He also notes that psychology cannot be a welfare profession, and students that wish to help should do so through the social work department. The first line of defense for reducing generalized anxiety disorder (GAD) comes from education, social welfare, and social reforms. Furthermore, the APA ethics codes are committed to the promotion of social welfare. The social responsibilities seen in Africa by Gobodo-Madikizela (2008) begins in rural areas. And to better the definition of rule, Werth, Hasting and Riding-Malon (2010) wrote that a population outside the urban center and these rural areas are isolated from the availability of mental health professionals. In Werth et al. (2010) article on rural ethics, it showed lack of intervention by psychologist that creates a void in the communities.

Ethical standards are being violated by individuals who wish to interfere with social reforms, which would enable the general population to overcome internal complex. It is unexplainable how nations, who state that their form of government, would lift the general population to a higher standard yet continue to cause chaos in the name of their god. According to Werth et al. (2010), the lack of qualified mental care of these rural communities goes against the obligation and violates the principle of no harm.

According to Gobodo-Madikizela (2008), "the behavior of individuals in clinical physicians violates the ethical standard of social responsibility when it causes harm to other individuals." It is important that HRDs take responsibility, regardless of their location, to decrease human rights violation and human sufferings. No HRD should take this as an obligation but should view this as a social responsibility to protect the general population. Psychologist Werth et al. (2010) notes are viewing and helping individuals according to their own financial gains. In view of the lack of financial resources, the workers in HRDs would be faced with a reduction of income when assisting individuals in the underpopulated area and cannot provide themselves the same income as work being done in an urban area.

If politician, educator, or human resource department had viewed their social responsibility and approached behavior to avoid violation, we could see a decrease in human suffering. "Using an online training program as per Werth et al. (2010), reducing course of education psychology, and requiring that they spend a part of their career or training in these rural areas could have a positive impact."

In each of the references that are provided, clinical social workers seem not to be a primary concern of psychologist, noting the decrease of clinics stated by Werth et al. (2010). The implication referred to also by Gobodo-Madikizela (2008), undermining those who should work only in the social welfare—established agencies rather than in their own practice would be improper behavior of a psychologist. When the US Military needed doctors and did not outsource but provided funding for individuals to receive doctoral degrees with a four-year commitment to the Department of Defense, we were better able to provide mental health care according to Johnson, Grasso, and Maslowski (2010).

One of the issues of the conflict between ethics and law and standards being violated is that many professionals were not able to separate Department of Defense regulation and ethical standards versus those psychologists/HRDs working outside the military.

The behavior that violates the clinical social workers is their inability to separate the legal conflict and apply the definition to military mental health. Clinical social workers that violate ethical standards, regardless of where they are assigned, creates a dilemma for those that are called to defend the country but are not given the same consideration as those who do not serve in the armed forces (Johnson et. al., 2010). The new APA policies prohibit psychologist from working in detention settings that are in violation of international law or the US constitution. Because the military deems itself beyond the legality of civil law and has its own system of discipline, this could be a conflict of APA standard.

According to Johnson et al. (2010), a better approach to afford behavior violations would be an oversight committee, which would be able to govern the behavior of clinical social workers. Throughout this paper, the areas of concern of legal conflict responsibility to society, social worker responsibility, and ethical behavior are directly related to mannerisms of responsibility of psychologist as noted by Johnson et al. (2010).

Each reference used in this paper noted the improper behavior presented in the paper.

To ensure politician, educator, or human resource department behavior is not circumvented as the paper has noted, the standards established by APA cannot conflict with the law. The question is, is the law written first, which prohibit psychology protecting the mental law of society, or is the mental health of the individual more important than abiding by the law that compromises APA standard? (Johnson, et al., 2010).

HRDs have responsibility to speak out. At what point does the psychologist have a responsibility to speak out? According to Barsky (2011), most major corporations have a human resource department, and yet people engage in unethical work behavior. It is easy to pinpoint the improper behavior by following current events over the last ten years. As long as politicians, educators, or human resource departments allow financial gain to take priority over moral issues, we will continue to have corruption in the workplace. It would be interesting to write a thesis of the beliefs of psychologist and why they do not take on the responsibility to speak out.

As noted by Johnson et al. (2010), "the hierarchy precludes moral interventions, therefore justifying improper behavior." The lack of properly trained human resource departments, that are to set ethical standards to ensure human rights are not violated, has to be separated from the hierarchy. "The moral justification of improper behavior and the lack of psychologist speaking out are directly related to their earned income from the corporation. When Christians participate and educate themselves and are responsible, they can hold these psychologists, the politician, educator, or human resource department and organization to a higher standard. Unfortunately, very few individuals have written on this subject or have spoken out against government intervention.

To avoid the violation of the lack of psychologist speaking out will take place when all denominations of all religions come together with an agreed upon group of individuals, which becomes the standard for the code of ethics for all people. The article written by Solbrekke (2008) encompasses code of ethics conflict legality, responsibility, social behavior, and speaking out. In this paper, the author showed a correlation between educating the community and individuals taking standard of ethics to the workplace. In Maslow's hierarchy of needs, the highest level is self-actualization. This concept of recognizing your own personal endeavors in many cases breaks down ethical behavior.

Education does not begin in grade school, high school, or college but in fact begins with the parent, which brings the moral beliefs to the school, which in today's society is circumvented by government regulations. Even though the paper by Solbrekke (2008) is directed to a novelist social worker, a student was concerned about the public debates in politics and the injustice in society. As noted by Solbrekke (2008), as professionals move into the workplace, the student now has a position where clients have an expectation of their input to go along with their expected outcome. No longer do we see professional responsibility directed toward resolving, enforcing, and implementing polices that protect the public.

In conclusion, what comes first, the income and well-being of the psychologist or the health and welfare of the client? The ethical dilemma is that government bureaucrats have established rules governing behavior, according to the government standards, which in many cases circumvent standards of a church. The reasoning behind my writing this article is to intervene and to help those with Christian background to not change their course but to follow God. Since my degrees are both in education and theology, I am giving a Christian viewpoint. The First Amendment granted freedom of speech, and the law was written so that the conflict in society was to speak out against unethical procedure; however, many pastors and Christian psychologists do not voice their disagreement for fear of reprisal.

References

Akfert, S. 2012. "Ethical Dilemmas Experienced by Psychological Counselors Working at Different Institutions and their Attitudes and Behaviors as a Response to These Dilemmas." Educational Sciences: Theory & Practice, 12(3), 1806-1812. Retrieved from http://0ehis.ebscohost.com.library.regent.edu/eds/pdfviewer/pdfviewer?vid=2&sid=f16f7.

American Psychology Association. 2009. "Ethical Principles of Psychologist and Code of Conduct." American Psychologist, 57, 1060-1073. Retrieved from http://www.apa.org/ethics/code/index.aspx.

Barsky, A. 2011. "Investigating the Effects of Moral Disengagement and Participation on Unethical Work Behavior." Journal Of Business Ethics, 104(1), 59-75. Retrieved from http://0ehis.ebscohost.com.library. regent.edu/eds/pdfviewer/pdfviewer?vid=3&sid =f16f7.

Gobodo-Madikizela, P. 2009. "Exploring the Ethical Principle of Social Responsibility and Other Ethical Issues in the Context of the Mental Health Professionals' Response to Xenophobic Violence in Cape Town." Psychoanalytic Psychotherapy in South Africa, 17(2), 73-95. Retrieved from http://0ehis.ebscohost.com.library. regent.edu/eds/pdfviewer/pdfviewer?vid=4&sid= 060177d9-.

Ivey, A. E., Ivey, M. B., and C. P. Zalaquett. 2010. *Facilitation Client Development in a Multicultural Society* (p. 248). Belmont, CA: Cengage Learning.

Johnson, W., Grasso, I., and K. Maslowski. 2010. Conflicts Between Ethics and Law for Military Mental Health Providers. Military Medicine, 175(8), 548-553. Retrieved from http://0ehis. ebscohost.com.library.regent.edu/eds/pdfviewer/ pdfviewer?vid=5&sid=f16f7.

Matusek, J., and M. Wright. 2010. "Ethical Dilemmas in Treating Clients with Eating Disorders: A Review and Application of an Integrative Ethical Decision-Making Model." European Eating Disorders Review, 18(6), 434-452.

Solbrekke, T. 2008. "Professional Responsibility as Legitimate Compromises—from Communities of

Education to Communities of Work." Studies in Higher Education. Retrieved from http://0ehis.ebscohost.com.library.regent.edu/eds/pdfviewer/pdfviewer?vid=5&sid=f16f7.

Werth Jr., J. L., S. L. Hastings, and R. Riding-Malon. 2010. "Ethical Challenges of Practicing in Rural Areas," pp. 538, 539–540 Journal of Clinical Psychology, 66(5), 537–548. Retrieved from http://0ehis.ebscohost.com.library.regent.edu/eds/pdfviewer/pdfviewer?vid=6&sid=f16f7.

>> cfabamerica@gmail.com, www.cfabamerica.com

Send your donations to your donation to your local charities.

Community assistant program (CAP) i

APPENDIX 2

Opening a daycare

Opening a licensed family day care home (FDCH) can be challenging and requires planning and preparation. Every FDCH subject to licensing must meet the licensing standards established by Florida Statutes 402.301-.319 (FS), Florida Administrative Code 65C-20 (FAC), and the Family Day Care Home/ Large Family Child Care Home Handbook, which is incorporated by reference in rule 65C-20.008. These laws can be found at https://www.myflfamilies.com/service-programs/child-care/laws-and-requirements.shtml.

Family day care home definition:

Section 402.302(8), Florida Statutes, defines family day care home as "an occupied residence in which child care is regularly provided for children from at least two unrelated families and which receives a payment, fee, or grant for any of the children receiving care, whether or not operated for profit."

Child care regulation in Florida:

The Office of Child Care Regulation in the Department of Children and Families is statutorily responsible, per Florida Statutes 402.313, FS, and Florida Administrative Code 65C-20, FAC, for licensing child care programs in sixty-two of Florida's sixty-seven counties. The remaining five counties—Broward, Hillsborough, Palm Beach, Pinellas, and Sarasota—have elected to designate a local licensing agency, per provisions in 402.306, FS, to regulate child care licensing programs in their area. Local licensing programs must meet or exceed all standards established for the provision of child care in the State of Florida.

To locate child care licensing contact information statewide, please click on the following link:

https://www.myflfamilies.com/service-programs/child-care/contacts.shtml

The five local licensing counties—Broward, Hillsborough, Palm Beach, Pinellas, and Sarasota—provide an additional link on that page for more information specific to their county.

Things to consider:

Business considerations

- Subdivision/homeowner's covenants—Some subdivisions have covenants and by-laws that prohibit the operation of family day care homes. Verify that there are no restrictions in your neighborhood or homeowner's association that prohibit you from operating a family day care home. Family day care home providers must obtain written approval from local government entities, HOA (if applicable), and/or landlord (if applicable) or a signed attestation, acknowledging their responsibility for compliance.

- Occupational license—Some cities and counties require an occupational license for the operation of a family day care home. Check with your local building and zoning department to determine if an occupational license is required.
- Rental properties—If renting your home, verify that your landlord agrees to this type of business.

Opening a licensed family day care home – December 2019 (1)

- Radon testing requirements—Florida Statute 404.056 and Chapter 64E-5 Part XII B require that indoor radon levels must be measured in licensed family child care homes located in counties designated within the intermediate or elevated radon potential areas. These include forty-eight counties out of sixty-seven counties. Tests must be completed within one year after the family child care home starts operation. These mandatory tests are to be conducted in accordance with Florida Statute 404.056, Chapter 64E-5 Part XII B, and mandatory radon testing protocols and reported to the Department of Health on forms DH1777 or DH1778.

- Location—Choose safe places. The Florida Department of Health (FDOH) is working to make sure that early care and education (ECE) programs are located in safe places so that children aren't exposed to dangerous chemicals during their care. Even if an ECE program meets current state licensing regulations, children could still be exposed to environmental contamination due to location and location history. Because children are the most sensitive population, they need to be protected against harmful elements. For a free environmental assessment of your home's location, email the FDOH Hazardous Waste Site Health Risk Assessment Program at ChooseSafePlacesFlorida@flhealth.gov, or call 877-798-2772. To find out more about choosing safe places in Florida, visit http://www.floridahealth.gov/environmental-health/hazardous-waste-sites/safe-places.html.
- Tax considerations—For information on tax requirements associated with operating a small business in your home, contact the IRS at 1 (800) TAX-1040.

To learn more about the program and make an informed decision, please review the information below.

Opening a family child care home
program (OPENH) course:

The Department of Children and Families, Office of Child Care Regulation is offering a new online course, Opening a Family Child Care Home Program. The goal of this course is to provide individuals with an overview of opening a family child care home program in Florida. Upon completion of this course, child care professionals will be able to

- Describe the responsibilities of a family child care provider
- Analyzes the need for a family child care home in your area and what services are needed
- Establish goals and a guiding philosophy for your family child care home
- Identify the operational requirements of opening a family child care home
- Develop finance and budget management plans for the program
- Identify elements of program structure that need to be developed

Additionally, 0.3 CEUs may be earned for completing this three-hour course. To access this course, go to https://

www.myflfamilies.com/service-programs/child-care/ and select "Training & Credentialing."

The following information covers general requirements only.

Basic requirements:

Several basic requirements must be met before operating a family day care home.

- Operator must be eighteen years of age or older.
- Operator must reside in the home.
- Operator cannot work outside the home during the hours of operation of the family day care home.

Opening a licensed family day care home—December 2019 (2)

- The family day care home operator must have proof of a written substitute plan to provide at least one other competent adult, eighteen years or older, to be available to substitute for the operator in an emergency.

Training requirements:

A license will not be issued until you have successfully completed all required training and passed the associated competency exams. The department's online introductory training courses are available on the department's website at https://www.myflfamilies.com/service-programs/child-care/training.shtml.

- *Introductory training.* Operator and substitute who work more than forty hours a month must complete the department's thirty-clock-hour family child care home training, which is comprised of the following five courses (passage of a competency exam is required for each course):
  - ✓ Family Child Care Home Rules and Regulations (FCHR—six hours)
  - ✓ Health, Safety, and Nutrition (HSAN—eight hours)
  - ✓ Identifying and Reporting Child Abuse and Neglect (CAAN—four hours)
  - ✓ Child Growth and Development (CGDR—six hours)
  - ✓ Behavioral Observation and Screening (BOSR—six hours)

Substitutes working less than forty hours per month must complete the following training by passage of a competency exam prior to caring for children:

  - ✓ Family Child Care Home Rules and Regulations (FCHR—six hours)
- *Literacy training.* Operator and substitute who work more than forty hours a month must complete a single course of training in early literacy and language development of children ages birth to five years. The course must be a minimum of five-clock hours or 0.5 continuing education units

(CEUs) and may be fulfilled through one of the following sources:

- ✓ One of the department's web-based courses: Early Literacy Birth to Three or Emergent Literacy for VPK Instructors *or*
- ✓ An approved literacy course (a list of approved courses can be found at <u>http://ccrain.fl-dcf. org/documents/-99/560.pdf#page=1</u>) *or*
- One college level early literacy course (for credit or noncredit) if taken within the last five years
- *Annual in-service training.* Once licensed, operator must complete ten-clock hours or one continuing education unit (CEU) of annual in-service training during the licensure year. For more information see http://ccrain.fl-dcf.org/documents/6/92. pdf.
- *CPR/first aid training.* Operator and substitute must be certified in first aid training and pediatric cardiopulmonary resuscitation (CPR) procedures. CPR training may be classroom or online instruction and must include an on-site instructor-based skills assessment that is documented by a certified CPR instructor. Documentation of the online course and on-site assessment must be maintained by the operator.

Opening a licensed family day care

home—December 2019 (3)

- *Safe sleep/shaken baby syndrome training.* Operator and substitute(s) who work in a home that offers care to infants must have training regarding guidance on safe sleep practices and preventing shaken baby syndrome. One of the following courses must be completed:
  - ✓ DCF Health, Safety and Nutrition (HSAN—eight hours) *or*
  - ✓ DCF Safe Sleep Practices for Child Care (SAFE—one hour) *or*
  - ✓ Early Learning Florida's Safe Sleep Practices (SSPELFL—one hour)
- *Fire extinguisher training.* Operator and substitute(s) must complete the training.

To learn more about training requirements, including online training, instructor-based courses, or to be followed.

- Operation of a fire extinguisher. This training is not offered by the department. Schedule competency exams. Please visit http://ccrain.fl-dcf.com/documents/-99/2490.pdf.

Background screening requirements:

The operator, adult household members and children twelve to seventeen years of age, and the substitute must be cleared through background screening prior to the licensure of a family day care home. The screening components below will be completed as part of your application process:

- Federal Bureau of Investigation (FBI) and Florida Department of Law Enforcement (FDLE). Required for operator, adult household members, and substitute. All electronic fingerprinting must be submitted and processed through the Background Screening Clearinghouse.

Instructions for registering as user in the Clearinghouse can be found at http://www.dcf.state.fl.us/programs/ backgroundscreening/docs/ClearinghousePortal _UserRegistrationGuide_DCF.pdf

Guidance on initiating screenings through the Clearinghouse can be found at http:// www.dcf.state.fl.us/programs/background screening/docs/Clearinghouse_Result s_InstructionGuide_DCF.pdf

IMPORTANT! Operators must initiate all screenings through the Clearinghouse prior to fingerprinting. Failure to initiate the screening prior to fingerprinting may result in screening delays, an invalid screening, or the individual may have to be refingerprinted at an additional cost.

- Out of state criminal record checks—required for operator, adult household members, and substitutes that have lived outside of the state of Florida in the preceding five years

a) The background screening unit is able to utilize the FBI criminal history results to satisfy the out-of-state criminal record check requirement for individuals whose out-of-state residency was in a state that participates in the FBI National Fingerprint File (NFF) program. A list of states participating in the National Fingerprint File (NFF) program can be found at https://www.fbi.gov/services/cjis/compact-council/interstate-identification-index-iii-national-fingerprint-file-nff

b) If the individual's prior state of residency does not participate in the FBI National Fingerprint File (NFF) program, an out of state criminal history record must be submitted to background screening unit for review. The results may be faxed to (850) 487-6030, emailed to bgs.outofstate.admin@myflfamilies.com or mailed to Department of Children and Families Background Screening Program 1317 Winewood.

Opening a licensed family day care home—December 2019 (4)

Boulevard, Building 6 Floor 3, Tallahassee, Florida 32399-0700. Nationwide criminal history record request information can be found at http://www.dcf.state.fl.us/programs/backgroundscreening/docs/BackgroundScreening-CHR-AHContact-List.pdf

- Child abuse and neglect registry checks—required for operator, adult household members, and substitute that have lived outside of the state of Florida in the preceding five years. Nationwide abuse and neglect registry record request information can be found at http://www.dcf.state.fl.us/programs/backgroundscreening/docs/BackgroundScreening-CHR-AHContact-List.pdf

- Sex offender registry checks—required for operator, adult household members, and substitute that have lived outside of the state of Florida in the preceding five years. For nationwide sex offender searches, please visit https://www.nsopw.gov/.

- Juvenile records check (FDLE)—required for all juvenile household members twelve to seventeen years of age. Request must be submitted online through the FDLE public portal. The ORI number FL721911Z must be used at the time of request. Complete instructions on how to request a juvenile record can be at http://ccrain.fl-dcf.org/documents/6/1019.pdf#page=1.

- Child care attestation of good moral character (AGMC)—required for operator, adult household members, and substitute. This form can be found at http://ccrain.fldcf.org/documents/6/78.pdf.

- Employment history checks—required for operator and substitute. A sample form can be reviewed at http://ccrain.fl-dcf.org/documents/6/324.pdf.

- Central abuse hotline records search (CAHRS)—required for operator and household members. This form can be found at http://ccrain.fl-dcf.org/documents/6/1005.pdf.
- Mandatory abuse and neglect reporting requirements form—required for operator and substitute. This form must be completed on an annual basis and can be found at http://ccrain.fl-dcf.org/documents/6/96.pdf.

Number of children allowed:

A family day care home shall be allowed to provide care for one of the following groups of children, including those children under thirteen years of age, who are related to the operator.

- A maximum of four children from birth to twelve months of age; or
- A maximum of three children from birth to twelve months of age, and other children, for a maximum total of six children; or
- A maximum of six preschool children, if all are older than twelve months of age; or
- A maximum of ten children, if no more than five are preschool age and of those five, no more than two are under twelve months of age.

Opening a licensed family day care home—December 2019 (5)

Additional considerations:

As a child care provider, you will need to consider these issues. These additional services are not required for licensure, however, to meet the needs of the families in your community this may be something to consider.

- Transportation—Prior to offering transportation services, child care providers should notify the local licensing office to ensure compliance with all transportation requirements. If you choose to provide transportation, you must have a driver with a valid Florida driver's license and valid certificate(s) of course completion of first aid and pediatric cardiopulmonary resuscitation (CPR) procedures. All vehicles, including privately owned passenger vehicles that are regularly used to transport children, shall be inspected annually by a mechanic, have adequate liability insurance, and have appropriate child safety restraints/seat belts. Additionally, a transportation log must be correctly completed by the driver and one other staff member and be maintained. We recommend taking the Department's Transportation Safety course, which provides information about licensing requirements and best practices designed to help keep children safe while passengers in child care program vehicles. To access this course, go to https://www.myflfamilies.com/service-programs/child-care/ and select "Training & Credentialing." For more information, please refer to the Transportation Fact Sheet located at http://ccrain.fl-dcf.org/documents/7/216.pdf.

- Firearms—At all times when children are in care, all firearms and weapons, as defined in Section 790.001, FS, must be stored in a location inaccessible to children and in accordance with Section 790.174, FS. No firearms or weapons, as defined in Section 790.001, FS, shall be kept upon any person located on the premises, excluding federal, state, or local law enforcement officers.

- Outdoor play area—An outdoor play space must be provided and must be clean and free of hazards and provide adequate ground cover or other protective surface around play equipment that is securely anchored. Homes that provide care for infants younger than twelve months only are not required to have an outdoor play area.

- Fencing—Fencing must be continuous with no gaps, and the bottom of the fence must remain at ground level and free from erosion or buildup. Fencing must have at least two exits, with at least one being remote from the buildings. The home must have fencing or walls a minimum of four feet in height if the family day care home property borders any of the following:

   1. Laned road or laned street open to travel by the public;

2. Road or street divided by a median and open to the public;

3. Road or street open to travel by the public with a speed limit twenty-five miles per hour or greater;

4. Lake, ditch, pond, brook, canal or other water hazards.

- Swimming Pools—Swimming pools more than one foot deep must have either a four-foot minimum barrier on all sides or an operable pool alarm. All doors and gates surrounding the pool fence or barrier must be locked while children are in care. If the pool exceeds three feet in depth, one person who has completed a basic water safety course must be present at all times when the pool is in use. Wading pools are prohibited. Please refer to the Family Day Care Home/Large Family Child Care Home Handbook, section 7.7, for more information about swimming pool requirements.

Opening a licensed family day care home—December 2019 (6)

- Pets—Animals, pets, or fowl must have current immunizations and be free from disease. Animals that are poisonous and/or aggressive in nature are prohibited.

Application:

IMPORTANT! Contact your local child care licensing office for guidance and further direction before completing an application for a license to operate a family day care home. Once all requirements are met, the application process will begin.

- Complete the application, which can be downloaded at http://ccrain.fl-dcf.com/documents/6/57.pdf#page=1.
- A $50 application fee is required for both initial applications and annual renewals.
- Mail completed application, including fee and supporting documentation, to the local child care licensing office in your area located at https://www.myflfamilies.com/service-programs/child-care/contacts.shtml.

Processing the application:

Once your application is ready to be processed, it will be assigned to a licensing counselor for review, if one has not been previously assigned.

- If the application is incomplete, it will be returned to you within thirty days. The returned application will contain a cover letter detailing the remaining information/corrections needed prior to resubmission.

- If the application is complete, a prelicensure inspection will be conducted on your home. It is expected that your home will meet all licensure requirements at that time. Should you fail to achieve compliance in any area, technical assistance will be provided and additional direction given. The inspection process will be repeated once you are ready to try again. Please note, you will not be approved for a license until all noncompliant issues are resolved.
- Once a complete application is received, it will be processed within ninety days. You will receive a family day care home license to operate once your application is approved, and all licensing requirements are met. If you are denied, you will receive a letter advising you of the reason for the denial and providing you with additional information on your right to appeal.

Upon licensure:

Once your license is approved you can expect the following:

- You will be issued a license for a period of one year.
- During the licensure year you will receive a minimum of two on-site inspections.
- No later than ninety days prior to your license expiration, you will be notified that your license will soon expire. A completed application for

renewal must be submitted to the licensing office no later than forty-five days prior to your license expiration date. *

- You must submit a new application if you wish to continue to provide child care at your family day care home.

*Reminder: Pursuant to 65C-20.008(3), FAC, failure to submit a completed application for renewal of an annual license at least forty-five days prior to the expiration date of the current license constitutes a licensing violation.

Additional information:

If you have further questions or require additional information, please contact your local office of child care regulation. Contact information can be found at https://www.myflfamilies.com/service-programs/child-care/contacts.shtml

Opening a licensed family day care home school

<h1 style="text-align:center">APPENDIX 3</h1>

Christian Philosophy

Christian philosophy: understanding and application of a biblical-based Christian worldview

Apostle Charles Frederick Tolbert, EdD, PhD

The First Amendment of Constitution states that congress shall make no law respecting an establishment of religion, or prohibiting the free exercise thereof or abridging the freedom of speech or of the press or the right of the people peaceably to assemble and to petition the government for a redress of grievances. Should politic debate moral and ethical standard? The purpose of this paper is to provide support for the politicians, church, and Christian worldview to invoke their rights of freedom of speech to follow the ethical behaviors of a Christian.

This paper is to explain and assemble ideas that can be utilized by citizens in America to further their Christian views, to take action against politicians and individuals who have falsely interpreted the First Amendment rights and Acts to Resolve Legal Conflict in any behavior by a politician, educator, or human resource department (HRD) that would cause conflict with the code of ethics should the politician's ethical responsibility conflict with the law. If there is a conflict, it should be resolved in a professional manner according to the constitution.

Ethical legality

God institutes human government. Apostle Paul stated, "Humankind is to be in subjection to the governing authorities. For there is no authority except from God, and those which exist are established by God." James Skillen revealed that Hartfield from the political system argued, "Is overburdened by the drive for power on the part of politicians and official. The power that attracts them is self-interested, parochial, and manipulative over against this degenerate use of power.

"Christian is called to exercise the power of servanthood."

Saint Augustine of Hippo had a powerful conversion to Christianity in AD 387. He was a Catholic North African bishop in Hippo. According to Michael Palmer, "Saint Augustine differentiated between human government and society (city of man) and the envisioned church to all believers (city of God)."

This was in response to the fall of Rome in the year AD 410: "If something is not of God, it will fall, but if it is of God, it will always stand. Saint Augustine viewed the church as spiritual and politics as material. This fulfilled the transformation as Paul described in scriptures, concerning submission to governing authorities. Let everyone be subject to the governing authorities because God is the one who puts them into position for all human good."

When an ethical standard is bridged, it has to be identified as a violation and brought to the attention of an ethics committee to determine the legality of the enforcement of the conflict entrusted between the public servant and the general public. If there is no immediate harm done to the general population, and this procedure does not violate ethical standards, there should be a determination on how to resolve it. The matter can be reviewed through legal counseling, where both houses and the citizens have the right to vote the politicians out of office. Unfortunately, there can be a conflict, which would not allow the government to fully disclose its breach based upon the rights proclaimed by the government for security reasons. The behavior, which violates a chosen ethical standard when there is a legal conflict, can be a line finely drawn. Many politicians are torn between ethical credibility and communication with their party or constituents and the legal consequences. By notifying the general public at the beginning of a campaign and discussing items which breaks any legal law or moral standard which has been reported, it is the first step of avoiding conflict with the public and the legality of the law.

Leon Howell stated, "The great issues of human time are moral–the uses of power; wealth, and poverty, human rights, the moral character of society, violence, etc.—indicate good but risk evil." However, God uses politics' method to accomplish his will. Christians should be obedient and good citizens. Only through God's work can they accomplish his will. In scriptures Apostle Paul pointed out, "For the creation was subjected to frustration, not by its own choice but by the will of those who subjected it in hope."

Politician's responsibility to Christianity

The issues Christians have in society today is, what is the responsibility of politicians to society, and how is this society defined? Michael Palmer (2010) said, "Karl Henry offered an example from the workplace. He condemned the assembly line that degrades men into machines and robs them of their destiny as Sons of God." David Sigurthorsson discussed the Icelandic Banking Crisis, how "it seemed to quite readily embrace the notion of social responsibility as contributing of their wealth to charitable causes—for example, to do responsibility as being about limiting risky and potentially harmful business practice."

Social responsibility extends beyond day-to-day work for the politicians, something good for another, and while paying little or no attention to the notion of social reform. The humanitarian responsibilities should be reviewed as a primary task of social responsibility. Society must see beyond their comfort zone, following Jesus's example. Practicing good character and conduct may help others change their negative thoughts to good. Michael Palmer said, "Justice or fairness means as individuals are judged according to their merits, not their gender, physical abilities, or skin color."

Ethical standards

Ethical standards are being violated by individuals who wish to interfere with social reforms, which would enable the general population to overcome internal complex. It is unexplainable how nations who state that their form of government would lift the general population to a higher standard yet continue to cause chaos in the name of their god. Laws violates the ethical standard of social responsibility when it causes harm to other individuals. It is important that Christians and other religious organizations take responsibility, regardless of their location, to decrease human rights violation and human sufferings. No politician should take this as an obligation but should view this as a social responsibility to protect the general population. Wendy Dackson said, "Christian church and society can never be separated. They are integral to each other because this is where people are shaped and characters formed."

According to Cornelius Plantinga, "Augustine found the one good that would not fade away, the one good that would not crumble if he leaned on it with the full weight of his love"

Ethics and law

One of the issues of the conflict between ethics and law and standards being violated is that many professionals were not able to separate department of defense regulation, the executive branch legislative and supreme court, and ethical standards versus those working outside the government. The behavior of the politician in their inability to separate the legal conflict and apply the definition to social welfare has been taken over by the government from those responsible in the church. Politicians that violate ethical standards, regardless of where they are assigned, creates a dilemma for those that are called to defend the country but are not given the same consideration as those who do not serve in the armed forces. Dackson explained the Magna Carta: "It stands mostly as an aspirational document. It described what for medieval England, good government under the king should be. It was a document between the relationship and the secular ruler. The Magna Carter can be seen as an attempt to reconcile with the pope and to at least give the appearance that good government is answerable to divine law" (p. 622). The military, federal, and state government deems itself beyond the legality of civil law and has its own system of discipline. This could be a conflict with biblical standard.

Throughout this paper, the areas of concern of legal conflict, responsibility, and ethical behavior are directly related to mannerisms of responsibility of elected officials. All individuals, which include Christians, have responsibility to speak out. At what point does the Christian's voice have this responsibility to speak out? It is easy to pinpoint the improper behavior by following current events over the last ten years. As long as politicians, educators, or human resource departments allow financial gain to take priority over moral issues, Christians will continue to have corruption in the workplace. The protestant evangelicals across the United States mobilized in defense of the Sunday Sabbath. Tim Verhoeven noted, "At the Lord's Day Conference in Baltimore, former President John Quincy Adams urged Americans to seize an unprecedented opportunity.

"The Word has never witnessed, 'He declared the spectacle of a universal obedience to the Sabbath." The United States could, as a result, be the first nation to benefit from the Sabbath's "full power to bless a nation" (p. 302). If Christians refuse to vote, they cannot blame God for its actions.

Moral justification

The lack of properly trained human resource departments that are to set ethical standards to ensure human rights are not violated has to be separated from the hierarchy. "The moral justification of improper behavior and the lack of psychologist speaking out are directly related to their earned income from the corporation. When Christians participate and educate themselves by taking responsibility, they can hold these elected government employees, the politician, educator, or human resource department and organization to a higher standard. Unfortunately, very few individuals have written on this subject or have spoken out against the government intervention. Education does not begin in grade school, high school, or college but in fact begins with the parent. To avoid the violation of the lack of religious groups, speaking out will take place when all denominations of all religions come together with an agreed upon group of individuals, which becomes the standard for the code of ethics for all people.

Christian responsibility

In this paper, the author showed a correlation between educating the community and individuals taking standard of ethics to the work place. In Maslow's hierarchy of needs, the highest level is self-actualization. This concept of recognizing their own personal endeavors, in many cases, breaks down ethical behavior. It brings the moral beliefs to the school, which in today's society is circumvented by government regulations. Palmer noted, "Maslow's hierarchy of needs that motivate behavior represents a major contribution to what third-force psychology is. Third force psychology stresses human nature and more philosophical and speculative than either experimental or clinical psychology." Whereas Steve Wilkens and Mark Sanford noted, "Christian community can be used by God to challenge others to take a deeper look at their convictional beliefs, especially when they can draw on the resources of Christians who are mature in their thinking and living."

Solution

In this paper, the author discussed responsibility of parents, politicians, and the workplace which are governed by laws voted in or voted on by the political agenda as Democratic or Republican other than by the people. When voting helps create a third political party, the other two political parties will form an alliance and come to agreements according to the need of the people. America is one of the few democratic nations which is governed by only two parties. Christians have to stop voting party lines but vote for individuals who are true believers in God.

Summary

If people's rights are being overshadowed by political rhetoric of security, and they continue to allow removal of the Christian teachings, they create a problem. They allow the decrease teaching of creation but allow the increase teaching of evolution. Those who are believers in God can only blame themselves. With over 90 percent of American believers in God, who can the Christians say are responsible for the lack of morality and either action of these politics? The people who represent Christianity must remove race, creed, color, religion, and even sexual preference from government's influence. The Scriptures noted, "They worship God in vain. Their teachings are merely human rules."

Conclusion

In conclusion, what comes first, the income and well-being of the politician or the health and welfare of the people? The ethical dilemma is that government bureaucrats have established rules governing behavior according to the government standards, which in many cases circumvent standards of the Bible. The reasoning behind the author's writing this article is to intervene and to help those with Christian background to not change their course but to follow God. The author is giving a Christian viewpoint. The Bible noted, "The Lord said, He teaches you what is best for you, and directs you in the way you should go." The First Amendment granted freedom of speech, and the law was written so that the conflict in society was to speak out against unethical procedure. However, many pastors and Christians do not voice their disagreement for fear of retaliation and loss of their nonprofit status. According to Steve Wilkens and Mark Sanford, "A lot of good results from political and social stability, military deterrence, and economic strength; and patriotism is properly directed when it acknowledges these positive aspects. However, to achieve and maintain power, nations must secure the loyalty of citizens, and without the loyalty power and state is in jeopardy" (p. 64).

James Sire said, "Ethics is transcendent and is based on the character of God as good (holy and living in a core commitment) Christian theists live to seek first the kings of God, that is, to glorify God and enjoy Him forever" (p. 132).

Most politicians enter into politics because of the increase of income and power. Many Christians respect power and money more than they respect God and their rights to establish a government, which allows the Bible to become standard operation procedure (SOP). Their lack of participation by religious groups for fear of other true believers to establish a political party can be viewed as self-serving. In scriptures, the Lord told his people to repent and if they do, they will enjoy a close relationship with him. That is the reason Jesus said he is at the door.

The writer's calling is to teach God's word to all the nations, concerning biblical responsibility. And the second responsibility is that the nations, to counsel those in distress and help lead them to a better way. God bless, America, under God for which everyone stands. In scriptures, "God rules the world, and he proved it by creating creation."

BIBLIOGRAPHY

Dackson, Wendy. "Anglicanism and Social Theology." *Anglican Theological Review* 94, no. 4 (September 1, 2012): 615–637. ATLA Religion Database with ATLASerials, EBSCOhost (accessed July 21, 2013).

Howell, Leon. "Theologies for Now: Concerns, Crises, Currents." *Christianity and Crisis* 48, no. 8 (May 16, 1988): 174-183. ATLA Religion Database with ATLASerials, EBSCOhost (accessed July 21, 2013).

Palmer, Michael D. *Elements of a Christian Worldview.* Springfield, MI: Publishing House. 2010.

Plantinga, Cornelius. *Engaging God's World: A Christian Vision of Faith, Learning, and Living.* Grand Rapids, MI: Wm. B. Eerdmans Publishing Co., 2002.

Sigurthorsson, David. "The Icelandic Banking Crisis: A Reason to Rethink CSR?" *The Universe Next Door.* 5th ed. Downers Grove, IL: InterVarsity, Press, USA, 2009.

Skillen, James W. "The Purist and the Apologist: A Look at Hatfield's Political Theory." *Reformed Journal* 27, no. 1 (January 1, 1977): 17–21. ATLA Religion Database with ATLASerials, EBSCOhost (accessed July 21, 2013).

Verhoeven, Tim. "In Defense of Civil and Religious Liberty: Anti-Sabbatarianism in the United States before the Civil War." *Church History* 82, no. 2 (June 2013): 293. MasterFILE Premier, EBSCOhost (accessed July 23, 2013).

Wilkens, Steve and Mark L. Sanford. *Hidden Worldviews: Eight Cultural Stories that Shape Our Lives.*

Apostle Charles Frederick Tolbert
Systematic Theology through the Spiritual Eye
Systematic Theology through the Spiritual Eye
Systematic Theology through the Spiritual Eye
SYSTEMATIC THEOLOGY THROUGH THE SPIRITUAL EYE SERIES
www.cfabamerica.com
amazon
BARNES&NOBLE

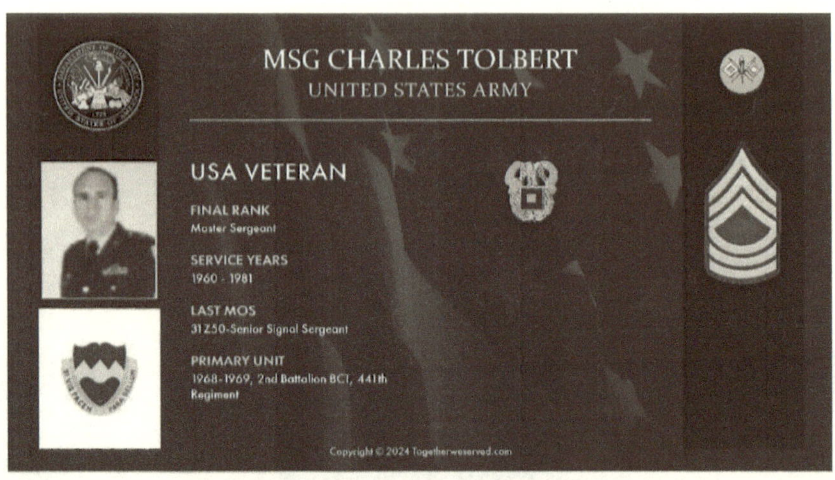

MSG CHARLES TOLBERT
UNITED STATES ARMY

USA VETERAN

FINAL RANK
Master Sergeant

SERVICE YEARS
1960 - 1981

LAST MOS
31Z50-Senior Signal Sergeant

PRIMARY UNIT
1968-1969, 2nd Battalion BCT, 441th Regiment

Copyright © 2024 Togetherweserved.com

Apostle Charles Frederick Tolbert,
DivM, EdM, EdD

Systematic
Theology
through the
Spiritual
Eye

Walking Your Vision University

NEED AT LEAST 4 BASIC
ELEMENTS TO SURVIVE.

1. Water
2. Air
3. Food
4. Light

AND LOOK WHAT THE BIBLE
TELLS US ABOUT JESUS.

1. I am the Living Water
2. I am the Breath of Life
3. I am the Bread of Life
4. I am the Light of the World

SCIENCE WAS RIGHT,
WE NEED JESUS TO LIVE.

When you think there is no hope.

God says, "Take my hand
and let Me lead the way!"

Aidan University
Upon the recommendation of the Faculty
And by the authority of the Board of Trustees, we hereby confer upon
Charles Frederick Tolbert
the degree of
Doctor of Philosophy
with all rights, honors and privileges thereunto pertaining.
In witness thereof the seal of Aidan University and our signatures are thereunto affixed
given at Jacksonville, Florida, U.S.A.
on this 24th day of June 2023.

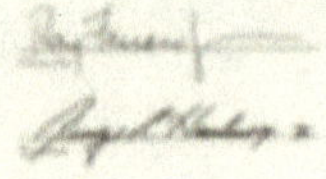
Nova Southeastern University
Fischler School of Education and Human Services
The trustees of the University
on the recommendation of the faculty confer upon
Charles Frederick Tolbert
the degree of
Doctor of Education
with all rights, privileges, and responsibilities thereto appertaining.
Witnessed with the authorized signatures and university seal in
Fort Lauderdale-Davie, Florida
May 11, 2010

arles Fr...rt, DIVM ED
Evange... ...olbert
W.CFACS.C... ...ALLTODUTY.ORG
...T FOUN... ...REATION S...

CFACS
Christ Found All Creation Saved, Inc.

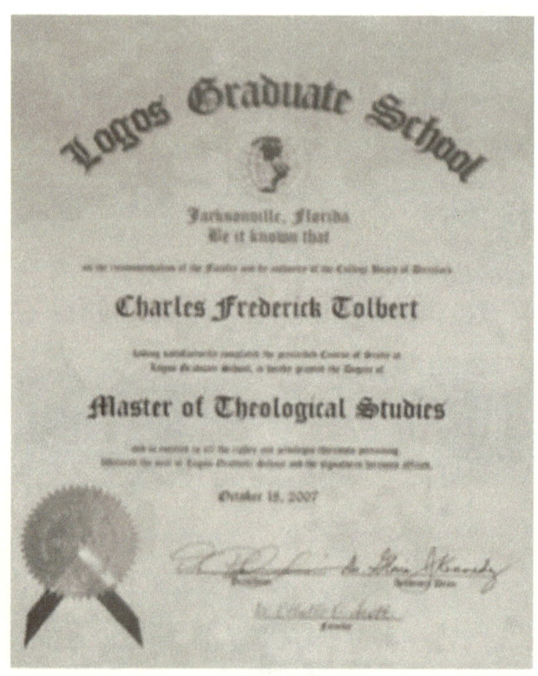

Happy
PAS OR
APPRE ON
Dr. L

ABOUT THE AUTHOR

Apostle Charles Frederick Tolbert, DivM, EdM, EdD, PhD, is a retired master sergeant in the US Army. He has a bachelor's degree in organizational effectiveness from the University of Maryland, earned his master's degree in theology in Logos University, master of education technology in American Intercontinental University, his EdD in educational leadership in Nova SE University, and his PhD in philosophy from Aidan University.

Apostle Charles Frederick Tolbert is currently teaching internationally in 45 countries with the long-term goal of establishing virtual reality hybrid schools in 195 countries.

www.ingramcontent.com/pod-product-compliance
Lightning Source LLC
Chambersburg PA
CBHW022000150726
47990CB00002B/536